Homemade SAUSAGE MAKING for Beginners

I0809172

Quarto.com

© 2025 Quarto Publishing Group USA Inc.
Text © 2016 Quarto Publishing Group USA Inc.

First Published in 2025 by New Shoe Press, an imprint of The Quarto Group,
100 Cummings Center, Suite 265-D, Beverly, MA 01915, USA.
T (978) 282-9590 F (978) 283-2742

All rights reserved. No part of this book may be reproduced in any form without written permission of the copyright owners. All images in this book have been reproduced with the knowledge and prior consent of the artists concerned, and no responsibility is accepted by producer, publisher, or printer for any infringement of copyright or otherwise, arising from the contents of this publication. Every effort has been made to ensure that credits accurately comply with the information supplied. We apologize for any inaccuracies that may have occurred and will resolve inaccurate or missing information in a subsequent reprinting of the book.

Essential, In-Demand Topics, Four-Color Design, Affordable Price

New Shoe Press publishes affordable, beautifully designed books covering evergreen, in-demand subjects. With a goal to inform and inspire readers' everyday hobbies, from cooking and gardening to wellness and health to art and crafts, New Shoe titles offer the ultimate library of purposeful, how-to guidance aimed at meeting the unique needs of each reader. Reimagined and redesigned from Quarto's best-selling backlist, New Shoe books provide practical knowledge and opportunities for all DIY enthusiasts to enrich and enjoy their lives.

Visit Quarto.com/New-Shoe-Press for a complete listing of the New Shoe Press books.

New Shoe Press titles are also available at discount for retail, wholesale, promotional, and bulk purchase. For details, contact the Special Sales Manager by email at specialsales@quarto.com or by mail at The Quarto Group, Attn: Special Sales Manager, 100 Cummings Center, Suite 265-D, Beverly, MA 01915, USA.

ISBN: 978-0-7603-9806-7
eISBN: 978-0-7603-9807-4

The content in this book was previously published in *Homemade Sausage* (Quarry Books 2016) by Chris Carter and James Peisker.

Library of Congress Cataloging-in-Publication Data available

Writer: Maddie Teren
Photography: Andrea Behrends Photography, except Shutterstock on pages 91, 97, and 99
Styling: Hannah Messinger
Page Layout: *tabula rasa* graphic design

Homemade SAUSAGE MAKING for Beginners

Recipes and Techniques to Grind, Stuff, and Twist Artisanal Sausage at Home

JAMES PEISKER
CHRIS CARTER

NEW SHOE PRESS

Contents

Preface

As both professional chefs and men who have plenty of knowledge about meat, we have created a slew of sausages that taste just the way they should (perfect), because perfection is what we strive for every day.

The purpose of this book is to give you the general knowledge and know-how for making sausages at home, either using the recipes we've provided or employing your own imagination. There is no limit to what you can create!

Porter Road Butcher is Nashville's only source for local, pasture-raised, hormone- and antibiotic-free meat that is cut to order before your eyes. As a whole animal butcher shop, we work closely with each farmer from whom our meat is sourced, and we take great pride in all of the products that we sell.

Although butchering is the foundation of our business, what we do isn't quite so cut-and-dried. Our skills extend further than just the butcher block. They extend to the sausage stuffer. And beyond.

When we started out, Porter Road Butcher was intended to be a small neighborhood butcher shop run by just two of us: co-owners Chris Carter and James Peisker. As a business powered solely by two men, we weren't left with much room to be creative. So we stuck to the classics when it came to making sausage: breakfast sausage, kielbasa, bratwurst, Italian, chorizo, and Andouille.

Along the way, however, business took off, and then for some strange reason people wanted to

work for us. Even stranger was that we hired them . . . and then shortly after that, hired some more. So we were left with more hands in the cutting room, and more brains in the kitchen, and therefore more and more sausages in the case.

Since those early days, our sausage repertoire has expanded to include a large number of links, in addition to pâtés, bologna, and our own version of pepperoni.

Although our sausages mainly revolve around **meat**, ingredients such as lentils, beans, and mushrooms can add meatiness to a meat-free link. In addition, duck, rabbit, deer, and other less common proteins can add an interesting flavor profile. Don't be afraid to experiment and push the boundaries after nailing the basics.

SAUSAGE /saw-sij/ – *noun* Highly seasoned minced meat, usually pork or beef, traditionally stuffed into the casings of prepared animal intestine or made into a small flat cake.

—*Merriam-Webster's Dictionary*

INTRODUCTION

The Magnitude of Meat

Dating back to Ancient Greece and Rome, sausage served as a way to use up what would have otherwise been discarded meat. By salting, or curing the meat, grinding it together with spices and vegetables, and stuffing it into the intestine of an animal, the Greeks and Romans were able to preserve meat and reduce waste—plus make something delicious.

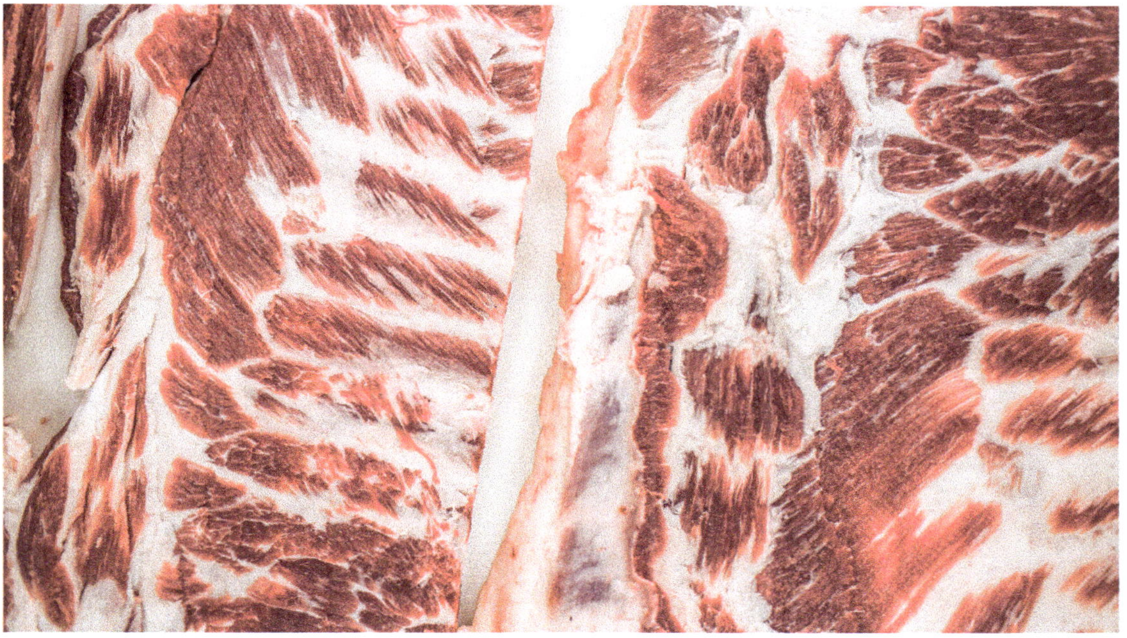

Sausage as Sustainability

In its foundation, sausage was about finding a way to employ every part of the animal instead of wasting it. From salami to loose sausage, pâté, and sausage links, making sausage all boils down to waste reduction and utilization.

Many people think of sausage simply as meat that is ground with spices, stuffed into casings, and then twisted into separate links, but unfortunately, those people are mistaken. Sure, sausage links are likely the most common and familiar form, but bologna, pepperoni, pâté, loose (unstuffed) sausage, and spreadable sausage all fit in to the family as well. Even a meatball is a quickly prepared sausage that home chefs make daily.

Today our knowledge of food and our efficiency of sausage preparation are a far cry from what the Greeks and Romans were working with way back when, but strong and steady remains the foundation of this culinary staple: **meat**.

Quality Is Key

By definition, the main, and most important ingredient in sausage is meat. So while this makes any cut or kind of meat eligible, remember that a high quality main ingredient produces a high quality final product: cooks are only as good as their starting ingredient.

A lot of people tell us, "I hate liver," when we urge them to taste our liver pâté, but what they really mean (but don't know they mean) is "I hate commodity liver." Ninety-nine percent of the time, when we offer customers a sample of our pâté that was made with liver from happy animals, their eyes widen, and they change their tune.

This is a flawless example of why finding excellent quality meat that comes from happy animals is paramount to making an excellent quality—and most importantly, delicious—sausage.

Finding a Farmer

Serving as the foundation of your product, high quality meat is ideal. No matter where you are in the world, the best meat comes from local, responsible, and trustworthy farmers who respect their animals.

So finding a reliable and responsible butcher shop, market, or farmer is probably the most important preliminary step to making sausage.

Animals who are given natural, drug-free lives; who are given real, GMO-free, organic food; and who roam freely on pastures as they were intended, offer the tastiest meat. By eating natural and wholesome food themselves, the animals are healthier and taste closer to what they should taste like: delicious.

Responsible farmers give their animals full access to the outdoors instead of locking them up in a pen lacking access to grass, fresh air, or sunlight. They don't pump them with steroids or hormones, they don't cause the animals to live in a constant state of fear and adrenaline, and they don't make them live in horrendous and unsanitary conditions. All of which means their meat is healthier, fresher, and best of all, tastier.

At Porter Road Butcher, we exclusively sell responsibly-raised, free-range, steroid- and hormone-free meat because of the quality of taste, and also because of the quality of nutrients. Animals that were raised in concentrated animal feeding operations (CAFO)—the commodity meat that you find at supermarkets—on the other hand, tend to be less colorful, less flavorful, and less nutritious.

What's more, commodity meat is often previously frozen, which leads to poorer quality. Because muscles (meat) contain ample amounts of water, water turns into ice if the meat is frozen. In turn,

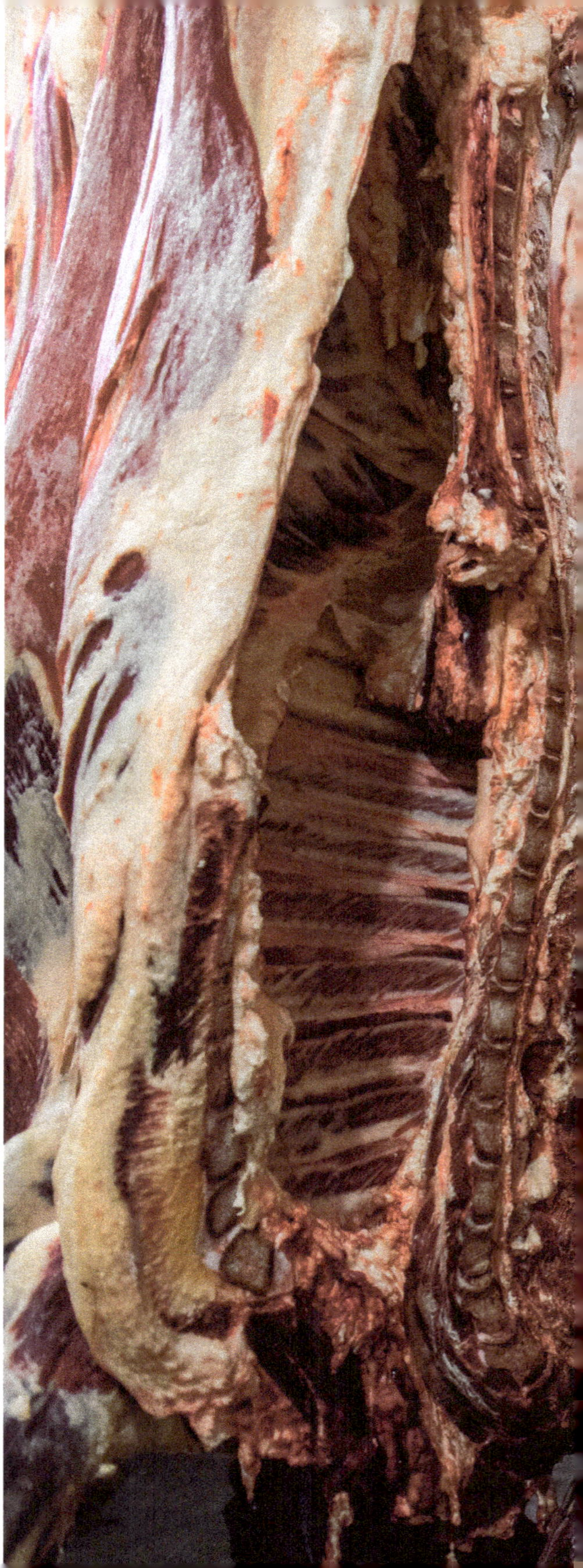

the ice crystals cut into the muscle fibers and loosen the muscle. Then when the meat is eventually thawed out, much of that water leaks out onto your counter or cutting board, providing you with a dry, flavorless piece of meat. No thanks.

As the foundation of our business, we've formed strong relationships with each of our farmers, ensuring that we know exactly where our meat comes from, and that the products we sell to our customers meet our high standards. Large-scale supermarkets and groceries neither have the same relationships with their suppliers nor afford their customers the same opportunity.

Although local butcher shops like ours aren't readily available everywhere, good farmers' markets and small local grocery stores are great options for finding local and free-range beef, pork, chicken, and lamb, among other regional meats. Asking sustainable or farm-to-table restaurants where they source their meat is also an easy way to locate trusted farmers. We're willing to bet there's a good one near you.

Making the Choice

Once you've made the choice to shop local and buy a product you can trust, then comes the selection: choosing which cut of meat is best.

In commercial sausage-making, large corporations generally stay true to the ancient idea that sausage should be made with leftovers: They use the buttholes, snouts, ears, testicles, and discarded scraps to fill those tubular casings and yes, they reduce waste by doing so.

Sure, that tastes fine. It even tastes good! But when making the stuff yourself, why not choose something better? For example, try an entire pork shoulder or a beef chuck roll in place of already ground meat, made up of God-only-knows-what. Not only does selecting a larger whole piece of meat give you more culinary control, but it also provides you with a consistent product.

Let's take a look at pork sausage, for example. In lieu of buying ground pork, which is a pre-packaged product that comes from upwards of thousands of hogs and employs all of the previously mentioned parts of the pig on one Styrofoam tray, use one large piece of pork instead. Dice it into cubes, and then grind it for a great finished product.

The bigger the piece of meat you start with, the more control you have over the end result because you can monitor what goes in and what stays out.

Fat Is Your Friend

In sausage-making (and cooking in general—but we won't go all the way into that for the sake of time and space), fat should not be feared. Fat is delicious, and it is a vital ingredient that adds both structure and flavor to sausage.

In general, there are two different kinds of fat on an animal: back fat and lower body fat. Lower body fat is a supple and soft fat that can be heated, rendered down, and turned into tallow (beef) and lard (pork), which are mostly used in cooking and baking, respectively.

Back fat, however, is not "greasy" like lower body fat, which has a higher water content and therefore melts easily. Back fat has a lower water concentration, which makes it thicker and more resistant to heat, and thus perfect for adding more substance to a sausage link. Those little chunks of fat also make sausage taste even more delicious and incredibly juicy.

For our sausages, we generally use the ratio of 70 percent meat to 30 percent fat. Usually, we just eyeball the ratio, so feel free to do the same. Proportions don't have to be exact.

Depending on the cut of meat you choose, you may be left with enough fat to satisfy the proper ratio in your sausage. If you find yourself lacking enough fat, however, you can buy back fat from your local butcher shop or farmer, and then dice it up and mix it in with the rest of the ingredients. In making chicken sausages, we substitute good, rich, European-style butter for animal fat.

So don't fear fat! Befriend it, instead.

Good Fats vs. Bad Fats

As we learn more about food every single day, we learn how various items are produced, what benefits they offer, and the problems they can potentially cause. In turn, conflicting information arises and causes confusion for consumers:

- Kale is the ultimate "super food." vs. eating too much kale will cause cancer.
- Red wine is fattening, filled with sugar, and bad for your liver vs. one glass of red wine each night is beneficial to your overall health.
- Increased intake of carrots will reduce your risk of cardiovascular disease and improve your eye strength vs. adding too many carrots to your diet will cause your skin to turn orange.

And who could forget the age-old favorite:

- Eating fat will make you fat vs. fat is good in moderation.

We're not doctors, we don't have PhDs, and we certainly didn't spend an additional four years in a university wearing lab coats and peering into microscopes. But we did learn a thing or two at culinary school, and we have been known to read books from time to time. So here's what we know about fat.

Although certain fats can make you fat if consumed in excess, not all fats are bad. Fat is necessary for a healthy and functioning body. Plus, there are many different kinds of fats, and the body must maintain a balance of "good" and "bad."

Most commonly discussed are the omega-3s and omega-6s fatty acids. Omega-3s are the "good" fats that are frequently sourced from seafood such as salmon. A less commonly known but equally delicious source, omega-3s are also available in high levels from grass-fed beef.

Omega-6s, on the other hand, are the "bad" fats that come from foods such as French fries and ice cream, but they are still essential to maintaining a proper and balanced diet; they are needed for building healthy cells and the proper functioning of your brain and nerves.

Our bodies cannot produce these fats on their own, so humans must get them from food. Plant-based oils, such as corn oil, contain high levels of omega-6s, which is why CAFO animals—which feed mostly on corn—are much higher in omega-6s, which partially contributes to red meat getting a bad rap for being bad for your health. Contrarily, grass-fed animals have a high level of omega-3s, making them a healthier alternative to grain-fed (like CAFO animals) or grain-finished meat (animals that feed on grass for the majority of their lives and finish their lives eating grains such as corn).

As humans, we need a balance of 3s and 6s, which is why we follow the motto, "everything in moderation." The ideal ratio is 1:1 or 1:2, omega-3s:omega-6s.

CHAPTER 1

Grind

Nailing the Basics

Like many labor-intensive exploits that take place in the kitchen, when it comes to making sausage, plenty of prep work is involved. Pay careful attention if you want to present a beautiful and delicious product. We believe the following four rules are the most important things to keep in mind when making sausage.

- *Pick the best meat; quality meat makes quality sausage.*
- *Always use fresh ingredients; they make a difference.*
- *Use the right tools.*
- *Employ proper technique.*
- *Pick the best meat*

Pick the Best Meat

Meat is the foundation of a sausage—or at least, in this book it is. So why would you pick anything other than excellent?

First and foremost, look for a local or regional product that is free of hormones and steroids and was given free range or was pasture-raised. That will provide you with quality meat that has better flavor and texture.

Second, use your senses: look, touch, and smell.

Look

Take a look at the color of the meat you've selected. The darker the piece of meat, the more developed the muscles are, and the more flavorful the meat will be. Take chicken, for example. Thighs and legs are darker, juicier, and much more fatty and delicious than its dryer competitor, the breast. Furthermore, meat with a higher fat content provides additional moisture in cooking, which is delicious and ideal for sausage.

Touch

Pick up the piece of meat and feel it, even if it's packaged. An ideal product is one that is fresh and not previously or currently frozen. So take a look, read the package, and find out whether the meat you've chosen has been in the freezer. Then feel the meat: You want it to be firm, but not hard. It should have some give, but not be soft or wiggly like jelly. Think about how *your* muscles feel.

Smell

Go on, give the meat a sniff. One of the best ways to check the freshness of a meat product is to smell it. If it smells even slightly off or has any sort of off-putting odor, pick a different piece. Of course, good, aged beef will give off a stronger and earthier odor, but your nose will naturally distinguish the difference between a sweetly strong beefy smell and a rank piece of meat.

Once you've selected your piece of meat, all you need to do is dice it up and toss it into the grinder.

Of course, if you don't have (or don't want to buy) a meat grinder, or if you are uncertain about grinding meat yourself, find trusted local butchers who choose responsible farmers for sourcing their animals, and ask them to grind it for you. But really, grinding meat is easy and fun. Give it a go!

NOTE

Because of the omega-3s in grass-fed beef, it can sometimes give off somewhat of a fishy smell! This doesn't mean that it is bad (unless it has an unusually rank and off-putting smell), but instead that it's a good and healthy piece of meat.

Use Fresh Ingredients

Fresh herbs, local vegetables, whole spices, dairy from happy cows, and eggs from happy chickens will make a big difference in your final product. Yes, it might cost you a little more up front, but the return on that investment will be so incredible, you'll forget all about your down payment. So go on and invest in the best.

Plenty of online debate exists regarding the appropriateness of dried herbs versus fresh, and the fight for the dried variety has been a strong and valiant one. But when it all boils down, fresh herbs provide a more potent, full, and longer lasting flavor that you won't get from dried herbs. The oils that fresh herbs release and the richness of flavor they provide is far superior to what the flaky, dried kind will put out, so do it right and go fresh. We promise you'll taste the difference.

Just like herbs, spices are much better fresh as well—meaning freshly ground. Certain recipes of ours do call for ground spices, but we always start with the spice in its truest form and then grind it ourselves using a spice grinder. This method provides fuller, stronger, richer flavors, unlike pre-ground spices that have been sitting on the shelves and releasing their delicious fumes into the nostrils of unassuming passersby. Plus, the larger grind and the non-uniformity of the ground pieces will provide for better texture and bigger bursts of flavor.

TIP

If the season is right, plant herbs in your garden or in a pot on your windowsill, and you'll save a boatload of money plus feel even prouder of your homemade and homegrown sausages.

Use the Right Tools

Making sausage doesn't require an extensive amount of tools, but there are a few essential items you'll need to get the job done properly. The best and most important tool, however, is one that you already have: your hands. Your hands are by far your most valuable instruments in the kitchen—particularly in the realm of sausage. So don't be afraid to get your hands into the meat of the mix.

Scale

That being said, a scale is critical in making sure all of your ingredients are measured properly, providing you with a consistent product every time. A small and inexpensive digital scale is suitable for measuring spices and herbs, and a packing scale could be used to measure larger ingredients such as meat.

We weigh our spices and herbs to ensure an accurate reading instead of using measurements with a tablespoon or teaspoon. As James always likes to say, "a pound [454 g] of bowling balls and a pound [454 g] of feathers weigh the same amount" but the mass of the two are much different. A tablespoon of bowling balls and a tablespoon of feathers are quite distinctive!

Meat Grinder

Beginning with a large piece of meat, dicing it down, and then grinding it yourself is your best bet for consistency and quality. But even so, how much cooler is it to go from points A to Z totally on your own? No matter which kind of a grinder you have or how mighty your machinery, grinders are crucial to making a sausage that will have a chewy and consistent texture.

A meat grinder can cost anywhere from $50 to $500, but the most important factor to consider is maintaining a sharp blade. When the blade becomes dull, it slows down the grinding process and adds heat to the meat as it continually and slowly pulverizes the same spot. That slow and hot pulverization will deteriorate the emulsification—meaning the equal distribution of ingredients (particularly the fat) and the overall structure—of the sausage.

Avid sausage makers might invest in pricier machinery that will last a lifetime while fair-weather sausage makers could simply buy the attachments for their electric mixer. It's up to you.

Spice Grinder

For better flavor in your sausage, a spice grinder is a crucial tool. Ground spices will suffice, but whole spices are generally less expensive and taste better, too. A coffee grinder will work in place of a spice grinder as well, but be sure to wipe it out thoroughly to remove any stray coffee grinds before using it for your spices.

Stuffer

If you intend to exclusively make loose, unstuffed sausage, then a sausage stuffer is obviously of no use to you; you can excavate this tool from your box.

On the other hand, if you're a link-lover ready to whip up some weenies, a stuffer is essential for stuffing the meat into its casing.

Both horizontal and vertical stuffers exist, but we prefer and recommend the vertical, stainless steel canister-style stuffer. They can be a little pricey, but a decent one won't completely break the bank; they usually cost between $50 and $200. Again, for the electric mixer, there is also a stuffing attachment, which works in conjunction with the grinding attachment. These are best used for smaller batches, and they require quite a bit of muscle power.

Use the right tools: (A) spice grinder, (B) scale, (C) horn, (D) die/plate, (E) plunger, (F) cap, (G) worm, (H) mixer, (I) blade, (J) arm

NOTE

Make sure your scale uses both metric and standard systems of measurement so you can use recipes from throughout the world.

An interesting note about casings: There is no such thing as an organic casing. All casings come from commodity pork, which means there is no way for sausages to be 100 percent organic. It's something we would like to change, but at this point in time beggars can't be choosers, and we choose to eat Bacon Jalapeño Bratwursts, just as they are. What can you do?

Casings

When you make sausage links, consider these factors when selecting a casing: the ingredients in the sausage, the grind (or coarseness) of the meat, and the desired use for the sausage. At Porter Road Butcher, hog casings are our most common casing of choice, but we do employ smaller sheep casings for hot dogs, and we use easily peelable synthetic casings for larger, smoother sausages such as bologna and mortadella.

You can buy many different types and sizes of casings, but we will stick with just two main varieties here: natural casings and synthetic casings.

Natural casings are generally preferable when making "dinner sausages," as in sausages that you'll be eating whole, like a hotdog or bratwurst. Although it makes some people a little squeamish to hear it, natural casings are, in fact, the intestines of an animal. Once cleaned and lubricated, the intestines can stretch and twist without breaking, which makes them perfect for stuffing and twisting into sausage links.

Casings must always be used fresh, and they should never, ever be frozen. If frozen, casings will crack and therefore won't be able to hold stuffing. If you find yourself with excess casings after making a batch of sausage, instead of freezing them, simply cover them with salt and stick them into the refrigerator to keep them fresh and ready for your next sausage-making adventure! Just try to use them within the next couple of months so they are still fresh and good.

Synthetic casings are made from things like cellulose and other derivatives of vegetable matter. They are rubbery in appearance and not recommended for eating. We generally use these for large sausages such as bologna and mortadella. It would be pretty frightening if any pig had an intestine that was 6 inches (15 cm) in diameter…

Poker

A seemingly simple tool that's very important, pokers are three-pronged devices used to poke tiny holes into the sausage casing, allowing liquid and steam to escape while it is cooked, thus preventing your sausage from bursting open. You could use a thumb-tack or sewing needle as an excellent substitute.

Sausages that are going to be smoked should not be poked. As the sausage heats up in the smoker, the fat will leach out of those holes and drip out, leaving you with a shriveled, fat-less, moisture-less sausage link. So don't poke 'em!

Smoker

Again, not all sausages require smoking. In fact, there are some varieties that we never smoke! But smoking your sausage is another great way to add flavor and further impress your dinner guests.

TIP

When smoking sausages, take into consideration the *pellicle* of the meat, a.k.a. the tackiness or texture of its surface, which allows smoke to adhere. If you use a freshly stuffed and twisted sausage that is still wet, smoking it will be in vain; it will not retain the smoky flavor. Instead, allow the sausage to sit, uncovered, in the refrigerator overnight to air dry, which allows the link to set and also allows the casing to dry out. This gives the sausage that ideal tacky skin, which will retain that delicious smoke.

Learn the Technique

Many steps make up the road toward delicious and flavorful sausages, and the journey traveled can often look intimidating—but it shouldn't! More so, it should look like a sweet African safari on which you are about to embark: very exciting, a little bit scary, but overall fun. By following our step-by-step instructions, you'll be cranking out all sorts of sausages in no time.

Step 1: Sanitize

The first step in making sausage, sanitization is crucial to ensuring your sausage avoids contamination. Particularly in a home kitchen, germs and contaminants thrive all over: on the counter, in the sink, and on improperly cleaned kitchen tools, to name a few. Make sure your workspace, tools, and most importantly, your hands, are all clean before you do anything. Constantly wash your hands and keep your workstation clean throughout the entire process to avoid cross-contamination.

Step 2: Chill Grinding and Mixing Equipment

One of the most important things to remember while making sausage is to keep everything cold. If the meat becomes too warm, it won't grind properly, which will ruin the emulsification (structure) and prevent both liquid and fat from absorbing into the meat. That leads you to a dry, crumbly, and less flavorful sausage, and that leads to sadness.

Refrigerate the equipment you'll be using to grind and mix your sausage for at least 30 minutes to allow it to properly chill.

Step 3: Weigh and Prepare Ingredients

Use your digital scale to accurately measure out all of your ingredients. Keep wet ingredients separate from dry ingredients until it's time to mix. Wash and thoroughly dry herbs before using and weighing them.

Trim your meat before you weigh it; any sinews, bone fragments, or silver skin you remove will affect the weight. When weighing meat, create an ideal fat-to-lean ratio of 70 percent meat to 30 percent fat. Once the meat is trimmed, cleaned, and weighed, dice it into 1- to 2-inch (2.5 to 5 cm) cubes, small enough to fit into the hole of your grinder. Return meat to the refrigerator after it's been measured to keep it very cold.

Step 4: Mise en Place

Literally, that means "to put into place." Before you begin grinding or mixing, gather all of your essential items and have them available and ready for use: grinding tools, mixing tools, ingredients, and so on. Have everything you need at your workstation, and eliminate anything that is unnecessary. The best part? Having all of the ingredients measured out and tools by your side makes you feel like you're hosting your own television cooking show. And that feels great.

Step 5: Mix Meat and Seasonings

Using your hands, combine the diced meat and other ingredients in a large bowl or container. Remember: your hands are your best tools in the kitchen! Make sure the seasoning is distributed as evenly as possible. Return the meat to the fridge.

Step 6: Grind Seasoned Meat

Assemble your cleaned and chilled grinder, turn it on, and slowly add meat into the feed tube. Be careful to not overload or overfill the grinder. Add the meat slowly, piece by piece, so the elbow doesn't overfill. If you notice any smearing or clogging on the die, turn off the grinder and clean out the die. Smearing could also come as a result of the meat's temperature, so check it out to make sure it's still chilled.

This is also a time in which you could grind the meat again if you are going for a sausage that is firmer and less crumbly. The more you grind the meat, the finer the texture will become and the firmer the sausage will be as well. Once the seasoned meat has been ground, you have the option to add liquid for more flavor or moisture.

NOTE

The majority of our recipes use a medium die for grinding, but check the specifications on each recipe before you begin.

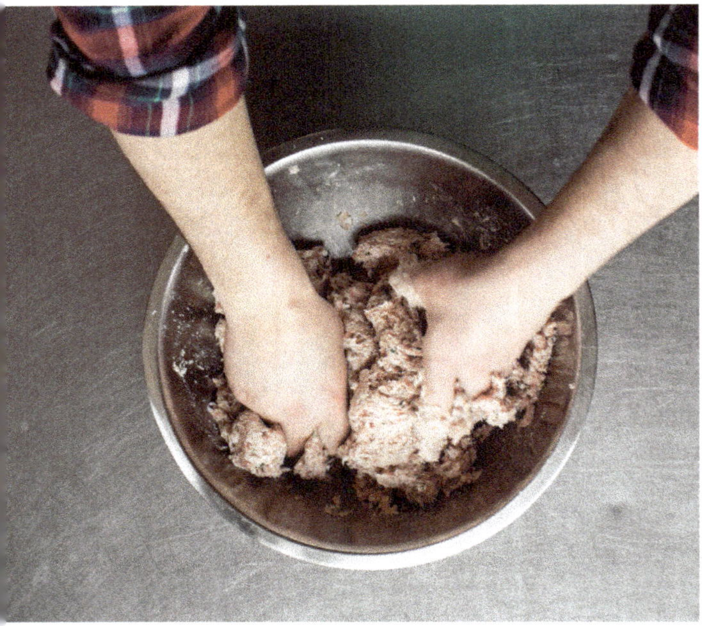

Step 7: Mix

Using either your hands (preferable) or your electric mixer with a paddle attachment, mix the ground meat and ingredients together. The more you mix, the firmer the bite of your sausage will become. Most sausages need anywhere from 2 to 4 minutes of mixing. You will know when your sausage is thoroughly mixed if it sticks to your palm when you hold some in your hand and then turn your hand palm-side down.

This could be the end of the road! If you are making loose, unstuffed sausage, then you've arrived at your final destination. On the other hand, if you will be stuffing your sausage into links, return your ground meat to the fridge to chill.

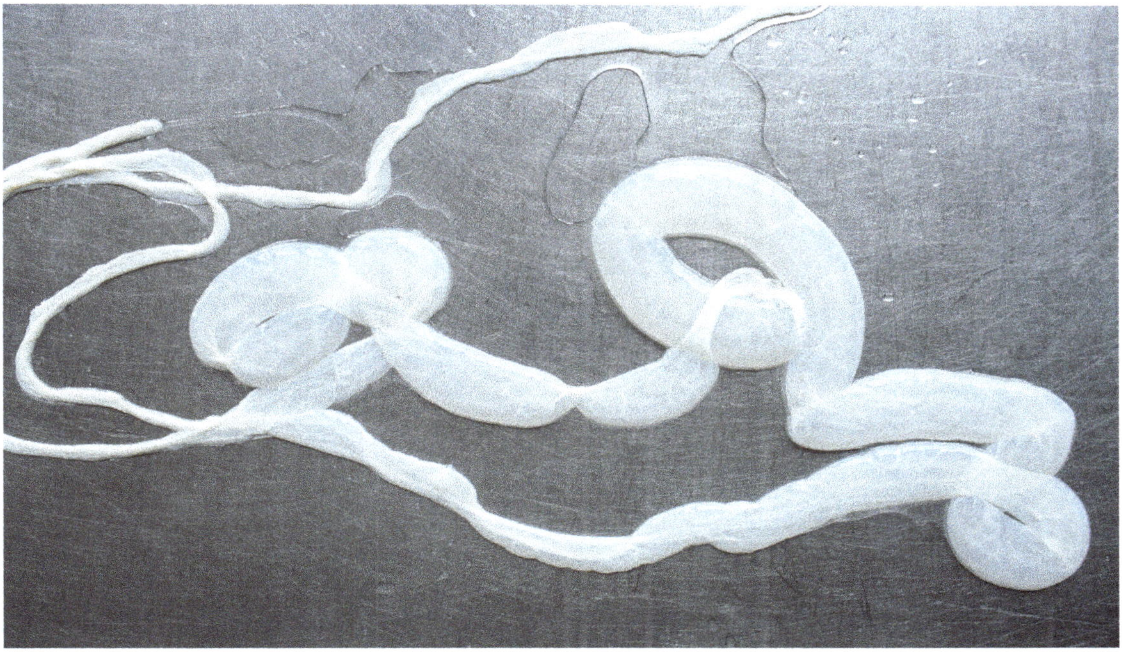

Step 8: Clean Your Casings

When using natural casings (recommended), soak them in water and find one end of the intestine. Hold one end of the casing up to the nozzle of your sink and, supporting the rest of the casing with one hand, carefully rinse the inside of the casing. Do this several times with each casing to make sure they are thoroughly cleaned and to check for holes. If you find any holes in your casings, cut those sections out.

Once the casings have been thoroughly cleaned, allow them to rest in water while you assemble your stuffing equipment. You can allow the casings to rest in water in a sealed container for up to one week. If you don't use all of your clean casings, just repack them in salt and keep them in the refrigerator, but remember: Never freeze casings.

If you are using synthetic casings, simply soak them in water until they are rehydrated.

Step 9: It's Time to Stuff!

Here's where the fun really begins!

Assemble your stuffer or stuffing attachment and fill the sausage canister with the chilled, ground, and seasoned meat. Press down and compact the meat to eliminate any air pockets.

Lubricate the feeder tube with water and slide the casing onto the tube. Once the casing is entirely scrunched onto the feeder tube, pull 2 inches (5 cm) of casing off the tip of the tube. Grasp the casing end with one hand and begin cranking with the other hand.

Once you can see meat begin to make its way out of the tube, pinch off the end of the casing so the meat is forced to expand inside of it as you slowly pull away, keeping a grip on the casing. Be sure both the casing and the counter on which the sausage will fall are very wet and lubricated to prevent any ripping or sticking.

When about 3 to 4 inches (7.6 to 10 cm) of sausage have made their way into the casing, let go of the end and use one hand to feed the casing off of the tube while the sausage is being cranked out with your other hand.

As you are doing this, be mindful about filling the casing. You want to find that sweet spot where the casing is filled with meat and a little amount of air remains, but not so full that it will bust when you begin twisting.

Once all of the meat has been stuffed into the casing, leave 6 inches (15 cm) of empty casing on the end and cut off any excess to reserve for future use.

NOTE

Casing can last in the fridge for 1 week soaking in water.

Fill the sausage canister with the chilled, ground, and seasoned meat. Press down and compact the meat to eliminate any air pockets.

Lubricate the feeder tube with water and slide the casing onto the tube.

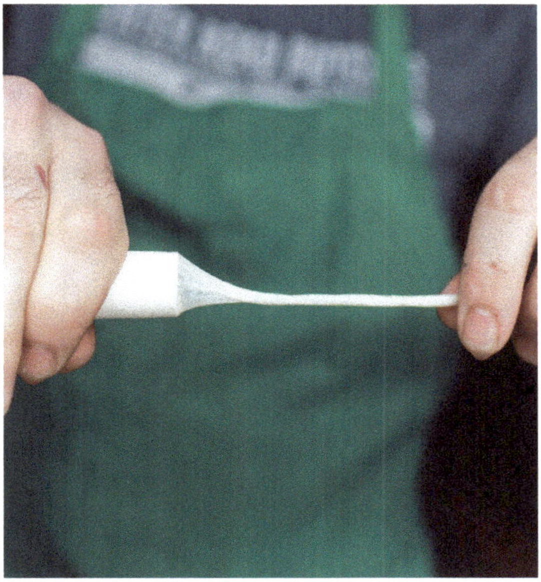

Once the casing is entirely scrunched onto the feeder tube, pull 2 inches (5 cm) of casing off the tip of the tube.

Grasp the casing end with one hand and begin cranking with the other hand.

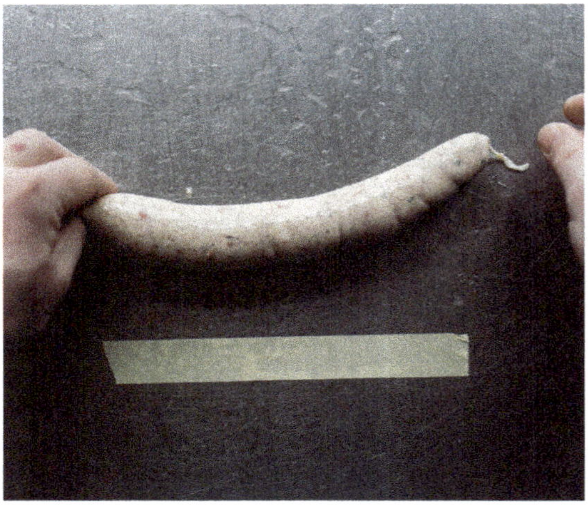

Measure the desired length of the sausage and mark your workspace with either a piece of tape or marker, ensuring consistency in the length of your links.

Then, keeping a hold on the pinched spot, slide one hand down to the beginning mark and pinch off the next length. Now, twist! Pick up the sausage, holding onto the two pinched spots, and swing it like a jump rope.

When you get to the end, tie it off with a simple knot.

Use a sausage poker to poke each sausage three times, or where air bubbles are visible. These tiny holes will allow the liquid to release while the sausages cook and prevent them from exploding.

Step 10: Tie Off and Twist

Tie off one end of the sausage and twist, making a simple knot.

Measure the desired length of the sausage and mark your workspace with either a piece of tape or marker, ensuring consistency in the length of your links. Starting from the tied-off end, use one hand to pinch at the appropriate length. Then, keeping a hold on the pinched spot, slide your other hand down to the beginning mark and pinch off the next length. Now, twist! Pick up the sausage, holding onto the two pinched spots and swing it like a jump rope. Repeat the process until no sausage remains. When you get to the end, tie it off with a simple knot.

Use a sausage poker to poke each sausage three times, or where air bubbles are visible. These tiny holes will allow the liquid to release while the sausages cook and prevent them from exploding.

As mentioned earlier, do not poke the sausages if you are planning to smoke them.

For best results, refrigerate the sausages overnight, uncovered, to dry out the casing. This will make the sausage slightly firmer to the touch and add ease for cooking. Snip the sausages at the twists to make them into separate links, or leave as a whole rope of links like those you might have seen in cartoons.

CHAPTER 2

Stuff

Making sausage doesn't have to be an exact science. Instead, it should feel more like a science experiment. Let's say you're getting bored of using pork as a main protein. Use lamb or beef or even give chicken a try. Just remember about the fat-to-meat ratio and compensate for lean (a.k.a. less fatty) meat when you substitute. In each recipe, we've offered the actual number of diameter that we use for grinding meat here in our shop, but as a home sausage chef, don't feel the need to follow every recipe so exactly. Any medium-sized die will do if the recipe calls for it (even if it's not exactly 1/32), and any large hog casing will work just fine in a recipe that necessitates it.

THE CLASSICS

Simply put, these sausages are classics. They're the ones that people count on at the grocery store, the ones that they eat week after week, and the ones that are recognizable, comfortable, and familiarly delicious. These sausages have likely made appearances on your dinner table at least one time before, they've been strong contenders for the grill at your family's backyard barbecue, and they might appear as a mere ingredient in one of your most famous recipes. These sausages are tried, and they are true.

When we initially opened the doors to our first shop in East Nashville back in 2011, these were the sausages that we selected as the residents of our display case. Our goal was to lure customers in using items they knew and trusted. Then, and only then, could we begin to steer them off the straight and narrow toward more unfamiliar territory. Because of the foundation that these sausages laid for our business, they hold special spots in our hearts, and we will always think of them as classics.

Breakfast Sausage

YIELD: 5 POUNDS (2.27 KG)/75 LINKS • DIE: 3/16 (MEDIUM)

Our famous breakfast sausage is notoriously delicious due to its bold flavor, hint of sweetness, and tantalizing texture. (It's got whole, toasted fennel seeds suspended throughout.) It's amazing! Although we created our own version of this recipe, the idea came from the popular store-bought breakfast sausage that is readily available all over the United States. To uncover the secret recipe, James took a trip to the grocery store on a Sunday afternoon with a pad of paper and a marker in hand, and took notes on the information on back of the package. Then he walked right back out of the store. After a few rounds of trial and error, we landed on this perfect blend!

1½ ounces (43 g) fennel seed

5 pounds (2.27 kg) pork

1½ ounces (43 g) salt

⅞ ounce (25 g) fresh ginger

¾ ounce (21 g) fresh sage

¼ ounce (7 g) red pepper flakes

⅓ ounce (9 g) brown sugar

⅓ ounce (9 g) ground black pepper

24–26 mm sheep casings (optional)

METHOD

1. In a large skillet over medium heat, toast the fennel until slightly golden and fragrant. Set aside to cool.
2. Dice the pork into small, 1-inch (2.5 cm) cubes.
3. In a large bowl, mix all of the other ingredients together with your hands until they are equally distributed.
4. Grind the mixture two times through a grinder on a medium die.
5. After each run through the grinder, use your hands to mix the ingredients together and fully emulsify the loose sausage. (The mixture should be sticky and well combined, and the sausage should stick to your hand when it's turned upside down.)
6. Form the sausage into patties or keep it loose.
7. If you're stuffing the sausage into links, add the loose sausage mixture to the stuffer; pack it down to remove all air pockets.
8. Stuff the sausage into sheep casings and twist links 15 to 1 pound (455 g). (Generally, each sausage should be around 2 inches [5 cm] long.)
9. Lightly poke each sausage link with a poking tool about 2 times.
10. Put the twisted links in the refrigerator, uncovered, and allow them to set overnight to dry out the casings.
11. Snip the sausages at the seams to separate into links.

Kielbasa

YIELD: 5 POUNDS (2.27 KG)/10 LINKS • DIE: 3/16 (MEDIUM)

A traditional, fresh, Polish sausage, Kielbasa is incredibly flavorful and is near and dear to the hearts of true Polish folks—particularly those who are no longer living in a country where it is readily available. As it just so happens, our East Nashville neighbors, the owners of a small, family-owned dry-cleaning business, are Polish in origin. Therefore, we knew they would be perfect taste buds on which to test our Kielbasa. When we thought we had it right, we gave the family a couple of links to take home and sample, and the response we received was overwhelmingly positive. So overjoyed with finding a taste of home here in Nashville, the grandmother came back to the shop the next day just to give each one of us a "grandma mouth kiss," as we like to call it. After an experience like that, we knew we got it right.

5 pounds (2.27 kg) pork
1½ ounces (43 g) salt
2⅓ ounces (66 g) garlic
⅔ ounce (19 g) fresh oregano
⅓ ounce (9 g) black pepper
29–32 mm hog casings

METHOD

1. Dice the pork into small, 1-inch (2.5 cm) cubes.
2. In a large bowl, mix all of the ingredients together with your hands until they are equally distributed.
3. Grind the mixture two times through a grinder on a medium die.
4. After each run through the grinder, use your hands to mix the ingredients together and fully emulsify the loose sausage. (The mixture should be sticky and well combined and the sausage should stick to your hand when it's turned upside down.)
5. Add the loose sausage mixture to the stuffer; pack down to remove all air pockets.
6. Stuff the sausage into the hog casings and twist links 2 to 1 pound (455 g). (Generally, each sausage should be around 8 to 9 inches [20 to 33 cm] long.)
7. Lightly poke each sausage link with a poking tool 3 to 5 times.
8. Put the twisted links in the refrigerator, uncovered, and chill overnight to dry out the casings.
9. Snip the sausages at the seams to separate them into links.

Italian Sausage: Sweet or Spicy

YIELD: 5 POUNDS (2.27 KG)/15 LINKS • DIE: 3/16 (MEDIUM)

Italian sausage is one of our favorite sausages to make for two main reasons. First, it is incredibly beautiful, and second, it is extremely versatile. When the ingredients are all mixed together, beautiful and bright colors emerge. There's vibrant green from the fresh herbs, a sharp contrasting red from the paprika and cayenne, and nice, bold flecks of dark black, deep red, and bright yellow from the various peppers. Plus, it's such an adaptable sausage when it comes to cooking that it works extremely well in a variety of arenas. We often like to leave it unstuffed so it can be browned and mixed into a pasta sauce, added into savory breakfast pinwheels, or even crumbled into a soup. Mangia!

5 pounds (2.27 kg) pork
1½ ounces (43 g) salt
1⅛ ounces (32 g) sugar
½ ounce (14 g) fennel seed
¼ ounce (7 g) coriander
⅞ ounces (25 g) paprika
Pinch of cayenne
⅞ ounces (25 g) fresh oregano
⅞ ounces (25 g) fresh basil
½ ounce (14 g) red pepper flakes
¼ ounce (7 g) black pepper
29–32 mm hog casings

NOTE

For sweet Italian sausage, omit the cayenne and red pepper flakes.

METHOD

1. Dice the pork into small, 1-inch (2.5 cm) cubes.

2. In a large bowl, mix all of the ingredients together with your hands until they are equally distributed.

3. Grind the mixture two times through a grinder on a medium die.

4. After each run through the grinder, use your hands to mix the ingredients together and fully emulsify the loose sausage. (The mixture should be sticky and well combined and should stick to your hand when it's turned upside down.)

5. Add the loose sausage mixture to the stuffer; pack it down to remove all air pockets.

6. Stuff the sausage into the hog casings and twist links 3 to 1 pound (455 g). (Generally, each sausage should be 5 to 6 inches [13 to 15 cm] long.)

7. Lightly poke each sausage link with a poking tool 3 or 4 times.

8. Put the twisted links in the refrigerator, uncovered, and chill overnight to dry out the casings.

9. Snip the sausages at the seams to separate them into links.

Chorizo

YIELD: 5 POUNDS (2.27 KG)/15 LINKS • DIE: 3/16 (MEDIUM)

"Chorizo" is somewhat of a loaded term because the word means different things to different people. From Portugal, to Mexico, to Spain and beyond, this sausage has incredible variance from culture to culture. Traditional Mexican chorizo is sold fresh, meaning raw and uncooked, and it incorporates plenty of ancho chile and cumin into the ingredient list. Spanish chorizo, on the other hand, is dry-cured and eaten more like a salume, alongside cheese or even on its own, with a strong presence of paprika. What we've come up with for this recipe is like a mixture of the two. We took our favorite elements from both Mexican and Spanish chorizo and combined them into one to make a fresh chorizo that is truly unique to us.

5 pounds (2.27 kg) pork

1½ ounces (43 g) salt

½ ounce (14 g) ancho chile powder

¼ ounce (7 g) paprika

¼ ounce (7 g) cayenne pepper

⅓ ounce (9 g) cumin

Pinch of fresh black pepper

⅝ ounce (18 g) garlic

¼ ounce (7 g) fresh oregano

29–32 mm hog casings

METHOD

1. Dice the pork into small, 1-inch (2.5 cm) cubes.
2. In a large bowl, mix all of the ingredients together with your hands until they are equally distributed.
3. Grind the mixture two times through a grinder on a medium die.
4. After each run through the grinder, use your hands to mix the ingredients together and fully emulsify the loose sausage. (The mixture should be sticky and well combined. The sausage should stick to your hand when it's turned upside down.)
5. Add the loose sausage mixture to the stuffer; pack it down to remove all air pockets.
6. Stuff the sausage into the hog casings and twist links 3 to 1 pound (455 g). (Generally, each sausage should be 5 to 6 inches [13 to 15 cm] long.)
7. Lightly poke each sausage link with a poking tool 3 or 4 times.
8. Put the twisted links in the refrigerator, uncovered, and chill overnight to dry out the casings.
9. Snip the sausages at the seams to separate them into links.

Sage Sausage

YIELD: 5 POUNDS (2.27 KG)/15 LINKS • DIE: 3/16 (MEDIUM)

When we opened our doors for the first time in November of 2011, Thanksgiving was just around the corner. We knew exactly what to do to get new customers in the door and to keep them coming back again, and again, and even again, so we gave the people what they wanted: classic Thanksgiving dinner sausage. When word got out about the incredible deliciousness of our Sage Sausage, a very trendy, local coffee shop asked us to make it for them to sell at breakfast, and we graciously obliged. Through both the coffee shop's support, and our customers' excellent taste in meat, Sage Sausage gained instant fame in Nashville. To this day, it is still one of our top-sellers during the holiday season, and we particularly like adding it to cornbread dressing or in the middle of a freshly baked biscuit.

5 pounds (2.27 kg) pork

1½ ounces (43 g) salt

1½ ounces (43 g) fresh sage

1¾ ounces (50 g) fresh ginger

¾ ounces (21 g) garlic

1¾ ounces (50 g) fennel bulb

¼ ounce (7 g) black pepper

⅛ ounce (4 g) red pepper flakes

29–32 mm hog casings (optional)

METHOD

1. Dice the pork into small, 1-inch (2.5 cm) cubes.

2. In a large bowl, mix all of the ingredients together with your hands until they are equally distributed.

3. Grind the mixture two times through a grinder on a medium die.

4. After each run through the grinder, use your hands to mix the ingredients together and fully emulsify the loose sausage. (The mixture should be sticky and well combined and should stick to your hand when it's turned upside down.)

5. Add the loose sausage mixture to the stuffer; pack it down to remove all air pockets.

6. Stuff the sausage into the hog casings and twist links 3 to 1 pound (455 g). (Generally, each sausage should be 5 to 6 inches [13 to 15 cm] long.)

7. Lightly poke each sausage link with a poking tool 3 or 4 times.

8. Put the twisted links in the refrigerator, uncovered, and chill overnight to dry out the casings.

9. Snip the sausages at the seams to separate them into links.

British Bangers

YIELD: 5 POUNDS (2.27 KG)/15 LINKS • DIE: 3/16 (MEDIUM)

Necessitating a little creativity in the kitchen, World War I brought on food and meat rations that were enforced across Great Britain, leaving every family with less than they were accustomed to. In an effort to keep some sense of normalcy at mealtime and to keep their families feeling full, home chefs elected to make sausages with their small portions of rationed meat and stretched out the portions by adding bread and cereals to the mix. When the sausages were cooked, they were simply put in a cast-iron pot and set on top of a big, hot fire. As they finished and were ready to be eaten, they would hiss and pop and bang around in the pot—hence the name, British Bangers.

5 pounds (2.27 kg) pork

1 ounce (28 g) white pepper

⅜ ounce (12.25 g) salt

¼ ounce (7 g) ground ginger

⅛ ounce (4 g) chopped fresh sage

¼ ounce (7 g) ground nutmeg

5½ ounces (156 g) dried breadcrumbs

29–32 mm hog casings

METHOD

1. Dice the pork into small, 1-inch (2.5 cm) cubes.
2. In a large bowl, mix all of the ingredients together with your hands until they are equally distributed.
3. Grind the mixture two times through a grinder on a medium die.
4. After each run through the grinder, use your hands to mix the ingredients together and fully emulsify the loose sausage. (The mixture should be sticky and well combined and should stick to your hand when it's turned upside down.)
5. Add the loose sausage mixture to the stuffer; pack it down to remove all air pockets.
6. Stuff the sausage into the hog casings and twist links 3 to 1 pound (455 g). (Generally, each sausage should be 5 to 6 inches [13 to 15 cm] long.)
7. Lightly poke each sausage link with a poking tool 3 or 4 times.
8. Put the twisted links in the refrigerator, uncovered, and chill overnight to dry out the casings.
9. Snip the sausages at the seams to separate them into links.

Irish Bangers

YIELD: 5 POUNDS (2.27 KG)/15 LINKS • DIE: 3/16 (MEDIUM)

"We like Irish Bangers because they are sausages that are similar to British Bangers except they are way better because they have lots of herbs in them, which make them taste good. British Bangers are good, too, but they are more bland and easy to mask with other ingredients in a dish. Irish Bangers, on the other hand, are really, really delicious on their own, or as a classic 'Bangers and Mash' dish, served with some mashed taters."—Chris Carter

5 pounds (2.27 kg) pork

⅓ ounce (9 g) fresh thyme

⅓ ounce (9 g) fresh rosemary

⅓ ounce (9 g) fresh basil

2 eggs

8 cloves garlic

⅓ ounce (9 g) fresh oregano

⅛ ounce (4 g) salt

¼ ounce (7 g) freshly ground black pepper

6 ounces (168 g) breadcrumbs

1 cup (235 ml) pork stock (see note below)

29–32 mm hog casings

NOTE

Pork stock is best if it's made at home from raw pork bones and fresh ingredients. Homemade pork stock has great health benefits and a wonderful gelatinous texture unparalleled by store-bought brands. If you don't have time to make pork stock, however, the store-bought variety will suffice.

METHOD

1. Dice the pork into small, 1-inch (2.5 cm) cubes.

2. In a large bowl, mix all of the other ingredients, except for the stock, together with your hands until they are equally distributed.

3. Grind the mixture two times through a grinder on a medium die.

4. After the first run through the grinder, use your hands to emulsify the mixture and fully combine the ingredients.

5. After the second grind, add the stock to the mixture, and then using your hands, mix the ingredients again thoroughly, until the mixture becomes sticky and fully combined. (The sausage should stick to your hand when it's turned upside down.)

6. Add the loose sausage mixture to the stuffer; pack it down to remove all air pockets.

7. Stuff the sausage into the hog casings and twist links 3 to 1 pound (455 g). (Generally, each sausage should be 5 to 6 inches [13 to 15 cm] long.)

8. Lightly poke each sausage link with a poking tool 3 or 4 times.

9. Put the twisted links in the refrigerator, uncovered, and chill overnight to dry out the casings.

10. Snip the sausages at the seams to separate them into links.

Garlic and Parsley

YIELD: 5 POUNDS (2.27 KG)/15 LINKS • DIE: 3/16 (MEDIUM)

We've reiterated time and time again the importance of good quality meat and fresh ingredients when it comes to making sausages, and our Garlic and Parsley Sausage is a perfect example of why this rings true. It's almost like a "poster sausage" for using quality components. The recipe for Garlic and Parsley uses a few simple ingredients, all of which are likely to be sitting around your house already, but the end result is something fantastic. This simple sausage link proves that by putting in the effort on the front end, not much work is needed to enhance the flavors. Simply letting the ingredients speak for themselves is the best way to show off the deliciousness.

5 pounds (2.27 kg) pork

1 ounce (28 g) salt

¼ ounce (8 g) freshly ground black pepper

1½ ounces (40.5 g) garlic

1 ounce (30 g) fresh parsley

Pinch of red pepper flakes

Pinch of lemon zest

29–32 mm hog casings

METHOD

1. Dice the pork into small, 1-inch (2.5 cm) cubes.
2. In a large bowl, mix all of the other ingredients together with your hands until they are equally distributed.
3. Grind the mixture two times through a grinder on a medium die.
4. After each run through the grinder, use your hands to mix the ingredients together and fully emulsify the loose sausage. (The mixture should be sticky and well combined and should stick to your hand when it's turned upside down.)
5. Add the loose sausage mixture to the stuffer; pack it down to remove all of the air pockets.
6. Stuff the sausage into the hog casings and twist links 3 to 1 pound (455 g). (Generally, each sausage should be 5 to 6 inches [13 to 15 cm] long.)
7. Lightly poke each sausage link with a poking tool 3 or 4 times.
8. Put the twisted links in the refrigerator, uncovered, and chill overnight to dry out the casings.
9. Snip the sausages at the seams to separate them into links.

THE OUTLAWS

Unlike the Classics, the sausages with which you are at least a little bit familiar, the Outlaws are sausages that you might never have heard of, or simply never thought to classify as sausages. This group of sausages makes up somewhat of a motley crew. Their origins vary, their frameworks differ vastly, and even their method of creation differs here and there.

The flavors and textures in the Outlaws are incredible. Some are new, and all are exciting, which is why we would never call them "the losers" or anything else that is similarly derogatory. Outlaws are law breakers, rule benders, and ones who fearlessly step outside the lines. They might be a little off the beaten path, but they're definitely worth the adventure. Take a walk on the wild side, and give one of these sausages a shot!

Kimchi Sausage

YIELD: 5 POUNDS (2.27 KG)/75 LINKS • DIE: 3/16 (MEDIUM)

Kimchi is traditionally a Korean dish made of spicy-sour, fermented vegetables. It can be made by slicing or chopping cabbage, radish, or cucumber, layering the vegetables with plenty of bold spices, and then putting them into a clay pot and burying it in the ground for at least a month to ferment. Our customer and friend Alan Powel is a farmer who ferments kimchi in large batches for us to use. When he first brought it to us, we didn't necessarily know what else to do with a giant batch of fermented and spiced cabbage, so we decided to make a sausage out of it! That's what we call utilization, friends. It took us a handful of tries, a bunch of tweaking, and even a deconstruction of the kimchi to get the recipe just right, but now it is one of our favorites.

5 pounds (2.27 kg) pork

1 cup (240 g) kimchi paste

1 tablespoon (15 ml) soy sauce

⅓ ounce (9 g) salt

⅓ ounce (9 g) black pepper

5½ ounces (156 g) roughly chopped cabbage

29–32 mm hog casings

METHOD

1. Dice the pork into small, 1-inch (2.5 cm) cubes.
2. In a large bowl, mix all of the other ingredients together with your hands until they are equally distributed.
3. Grind the mixture two times through a grinder on a medium die.
4. After each run through the grinder, use your hands to mix the ingredients together and fully emulsify the loose sausage. (The mixture should be sticky and well combined and should stick to your hand when it's turned upside down.)
5. Add the loose sausage mixture to the stuffer; pack it down to remove all of the air pockets.
6. Stuff the sausage into the hog casings and twist links 3 to 1 pound (455 g). (Generally, each sausage should be 5 to 6 inches [13 to 15 cm] long.)
7. Lightly poke each sausage link with a poking tool 3 or 4 times.
8. Put the twisted links in the refrigerator, uncovered, and chill overnight to dry out the casings.
9. Snip the sausages at the seams to separate them into links.

Potato Sausage

YIELD: 4 POUNDS (1.8 KG)/12 LINKS DIE: 3/16 (MEDIUM)

When James told fellow St. Louis chef Kevin Nashan that he and his new business partner were planning to open a butcher shop in Nashville, the James Beard–celebrated chef Nashan was eager to offer help. He handed over a 2-inch (5 cm) thick stack of papers, each one stamped with a recipe that he'd collected throughout his successful career. Nashan had learned a thing or two in his day, and he was eager to pass along some knowledge. Potato Sausage was the first recipe we tried out of his stack of hundreds.

1½ pounds (680 kg) potatoes
4 pounds (1.8 kg) pork
1 ounce (28 g) salt
¼ ounce (7 g) black pepper
⅛ ounce (4 g) red pepper flakes
½ ounce (14 g) sugar
2 cloves garlic
½ cup (120 ml) white wine
29–32 mm hog casings

METHOD

1. Add the potatoes to a stockpot and cover them with cool water by 2 inches (5 cm). Boil the potatoes until tender, about 15 minutes. Drain and cool. Pinch one end of a potato with all your fingers to pull the skin off and dice into small cubes. Repeat with the remaining potatoes and set aside. As the potatoes are boiling, dice the pork into small, 1-inch (2.5 cm) cubes. Return it to the refrigerator.

2. In a large bowl, mix all of the ingredients, except for the wine and potatoes, together with your hands.

3. Grind the mixed ingredients twice through a grinder on a medium die.

4. After each run through the grinder, mix the ingredients together with your hands to fully emulsify the loose sausage. (The mixture should be sticky and well combined and should stick to your hand when it's turned upside down.)

5. Add the wine and potatoes and use your hands to incorporate them. Mix the ingredients thoroughly until they are evenly blended.

6. Add the loose sausage mixture into the stuffing canister; pack it down to remove any air pockets.

7. Stuff the sausage into the hog casings and twist links 3 to 1 pound (455 g). (Generally, each sausage should be 5 to 6 inches [13 to 15 cm] long.)

8. Lightly poke each sausage link with a poking tool 3 or 4 times.

9. Put the links in the refrigerator, uncovered, and chill overnight to dry out the casings.

10. Snip the sausage at the seams to separate it into links.

Beef Bologna

YIELD: 10 POUNDS (4.5 KG)/1 LOG • DIE: ⅛ (SMALL)

As whole animal butchers, we've learned that every part of the animal can be put to use because throwing meat away is like throwing money into the trash—it hurts. When breaking down beef, for example, we extract all of the prime cuts first; then we dice down the rest of the meat and turn it into ground beef; and finally, we roast the bones and use them for stock and render down the fat to make into tallow. But what about those fatty pieces of trim that are pushed to the side during the breakdown of the beef, you ask? Well, we make it into bologna, of course!

10 pounds (4.5 kg) fatty beef
2 ounces (56 g) salt
1 ounce (28 g) pink salt
½ ounce (14 g) black pepper
½ ounce (14 g) white pepper
½ ounce (14 g) nutmeg
⅓ ounce (10 g) coriander
Pinch of dried bay leaves
½ ounce (16 g) garlic
Synthetic casings

METHOD

1. Dice the fatty beef into 1-inch (2.5 cm) cubes.

2. In a bowl, mix the salts together to create a cure. In a large bowl, toss the beef in the salt mixture, covering each piece. Put the beef in the fridge and cure it for two days.

3. Remove beef from the fridge and using your hands, mix it together with in a bowl with the remaining ingredients.

4. Grind the mixed ingredients four times through a grinder on a small die. Keep the mixture very cold while grinding. If the meat begins to lose its chill, return it to the refrigerator before continuing to grind it.

5. Using the largest sausage horn on your sausage stuffer, stuff the ground meat into a bologna casing and tie it off at the end.

6. Create a large water bath big enough to submerge the entire bologna roll, and bring the water temperature up to 150°F (70°C). Note: Use a circulator to help maintain the water temperature.

Cook the bologna for 6 hours or until the internal temperature reaches 150°F (70°C). Or fill a slow cooker with water and set it to the highest setting. Submerge the bologna and tie the ends tightly to prevent water from seeping inside. Remove the bologna from the water and put it directly into a large bowl of ice water to stop the cooking process.

7. Let the bologna cool completely before removing the casing and/or slicing it.

Cotechino

YIELD: 4 POUNDS (1.8 KG)/8 LINKS • DIE FOR PORK MEAT: 3/16 (MEDIUM)
DIE FOR PORK SKIN: 3/8 (LARGE)

Pronounced koh-te-KEEN-oh, this Italian-in-origin sausage is a common mealtime staple at New Year's and served alongside lentils, which promise money and prosperity in the New Year. Dating as far back as the 1500s, incorporating the skin of the hog into this sausage was thought of as a great way to use scraps and reduce waste. Fortunately, because the skin is so gelatinous, and because we grind it on a larger diameter than the actual pork meat, the larger hunks of gelatinous skin add a great chewy texture and a good supply of fat to the sausage. That's why this sausage is so succulent and tasty. Who wouldn't want to ring in the New Year with something as good as this?

4 pounds (1.8 kg) pork
1 pound (453 g) pork skin
2 ounces (56 g) salt
¼ ounce (7 g) black pepper
Pinch of coriander
Pinch of cloves
Pinch of cayenne
Pinch of allspice
⅜ ounce (11 g) sugar
Pinch of nutmeg
29–32 mm hog casings

METHOD

1. Dice the pork into small, 1-inch (2.5 cm) cubes.

2. Separately, dice the pork skin into small, 1-inch (2.5 cm) pieces.

3. In a large bowl, mix all of the ingredients, except for the pork skin, together with your hands.

4. Run the pork skin through a grinder once, using a large die. Set aside.

5. Grind the mixed ingredients two times through a grinder on a medium die.

6. After each run through the grinder, use your hands to mix the ingredients together and fully emulsify the loose sausage. (The mixture should be sticky and well combined and should stick to your hand when it's turned upside down.)

7. Add the ground pork skin and use your hands to incorporate it. Mix the ingredients thoroughly until they are evenly blended.

8. Add the loose sausage mixture into the stuffing canister; pack it down to remove any air pockets.

9. Stuff the sausage into the hog casings and twist links 3 to 1 pound (455 g). (Generally, each sausage should be 5 to 6 inches [13 to 15 cm] long.)

10. Lightly poke each sausage link with a poking tool 3 or 4 times.

11. Put the links in the refrigerator, uncovered, and chill overnight.

12. Snip the sausages at the seams to separate them into links.

Chicken and Herb Sausage

YIELD: 5 POUNDS (2.27 KG)/15 • LINKS DIE: 3/16 (MEDIUM)

Because chicken is naturally a very lean animal in comparison to say, pork, it doesn't leave a whole lot of fat for us to incorporate into sausage. As a way to integrate fat back into the meat and aid in emulsification, moisture, and deliciousness, we add butter. After all, butter makes everything better. One of our favorite things about Chicken and Herb Sausage is its deceptive nature. Because people think of chicken as a lean and healthy choice for meat, Chicken and Herb Sausage automatically falls into that category as well. Little do they know that part of the reason this link is so good is because of the buttery deliciousness that is mixed throughout. Oopsie!

4½ pounds (2 kg) chicken, preferably boneless, skinless thighs

½ pound (227 g) butter

1½ ounces (43 g) salt

¼ ounce (7 g) black pepper

⅜ ounce (11 g) parsley

⅜ ounce (11 g) fresh chives

¼ ounce (7 g) fresh tarragon

¼ ounce (7 g) fresh oregano

¾ ounce (21 g) garlic

29–32 mm hog casings

METHOD

1. Dice the chicken into small, 1-inch (2.5 cm) cubes.
2. Cube the butter into small, ½-inch (1.25 cm) cubes.
3. In a large bowl, mix all of the ingredients together with your hands until they are equally distributed.
4. Grind the mixture two times through a grinder on a medium die.
5. After each run through the grinder, use your hands to mix the ingredients together and fully emulsify the loose sausage. (The mixture should be sticky and well combined and should stick to your hand when it's turned upside down.)
6. Add the loose sausage mixture to the stuffer; pack it down to remove all the air pockets.
7. Stuff the sausage into the hog casings and twist links 3 to 1 pound (455 g). (Generally, each sausage should be 5 to 6 inches [13 to 15 cm] long.)
8. Lightly poke each sausage link with a poking tool 3 or 4 times.
9. Put the twisted links in the refrigerator, uncovered, and chill overnight to dry out the casings.
10. Snip the sausages at the seams to separate them into links.

Asian Sausage

YIELD: 5 POUNDS (2.27 KG)/15 • LINKS DIE: 3/16 (MEDIUM)

After being hired at the shop and working as a counter clerk for a couple weeks, Chad Curtis quickly became the number one fan of our PRB Beef Jerky. Since the job of marinating and dehydrating meat fell to him, the list of ingredients that made up said delicious jerky was soon memorized, and when he was promoted to sausage maker, an idea was born. Chad knew that the Asian-style flavors that made up the jerky would translate to a dynamite sausage, so he ran his idea past the rest of the team, and together they came up with a trial batch. After changing some of the ingredients from the powdered variety to fresh and adjusting salt levels, the Asian Sausage was officially born and further became a staff favorite. This sausage goes wonderfully with rice, mixed with vegetables in a stir-fry, or crumbled and stuffed into a lettuce wrap.

5 pounds (2.27 kg) pork
¾ ounce (21 g) salt
⅞ ounce (25 g) fresh ginger
¾ ounce (21 g) garlic
⅓ ounce (9 g) wasabi powder
1⅛ ounces (32 g) sugar
1⅛ ounces (32 g) sesame seeds
¼ ounce (7 g) red pepper flakes
2¼ ounces (64 g) scallions
4½ ounces (118 ml) soy sauce
29–32 mm hog casings

METHOD

1. Dice the pork into small, 1-inch (2.5 cm) cubes.

2. In a large bowl, mix all of the ingredients, except for the scallions and soy sauce, together with your hands until they are equally distributed.

3. Grind the mixture through a grinder one time on medium die. Add the soy sauce and mix into the meat with your hands until it is emulsified.

4. Grind the mixture again through a grinder on a medium die. Add the scallions, mix the ingredients together with your hands until the scallions are evenly distributed and the mixture is emulsified. (The mixture should be sticky and well combined and should stick to your hand when it's turned upside down.)

5. Add the loose sausage mixture to the stuffer; pack it down to remove all of the air pockets.

6. Stuff the sausage into the hog casings and twist links 3 to 1 pound (455 g). (Generally, each sausage should be 5 to 6 inches [13 to 15 cm] long.)

7. Lightly poke each sausage link with a poking tool 3 or 4 times.

8. Put the twisted links in the refrigerator, uncovered, and chill overnight to dry out the casings.

9. Snip the sausages at the seams to separate them into links.

THE WURST

Contrary to how it may sound, "The Wurst" are most certainly not the worst of the sausages in our repertoire. Who would actually qualify a group like that in a book for other people to read? Conversely, these sausages are some of the best-selling and best tasting links that we've got up our sleeves.

While the presence of "wurst" in each name hints at a group of similar products with only slight variation, the variance among this group is quite pleasantly distinct. The South African Boerewors are beef-based, un-twisted sausages that are presented in a long, curving coil, the Currywurst are slightly sweet and cinnamon-scented and would make for an excellent Christmastime addition, and even though neither of us comes from the northern Midwest, we've been told that our Bratwursts blow anything from Milwaukee out of the water. Just sayin'... We hope you agree that ours are the best wursts ever.

Bratwurst

YIELD: 5 POUNDS (2.27 KG)/15 • LINKS DIE: 3/16 (MEDIUM)

When master chef and charcuterie genius Brian Polcyn traveled to Nashville to teach a class about charcuterie and sausages, we jumped at the opportunity to attend. Already hugging his James Beard–nominated book *Charcuterie* near and dear to our hearts, we were thrilled with the opportunity to learn firsthand about technique and spend the day with a culinary stud. We have since adopted his bratwurst recipe as our own, and our customers have absolutely fallen in love with it, calling it the best bratwurst they've ever had. What's more, we've even improved the recipe by using our farm fresh pork, free-range local eggs, and incredibly rich, locally made cream. We're certain that it's those simple tweaks that make our bratwurst stand out among the rest.

5 pounds (2.27 kg) pork
1¾ ounces (50 g) salt
¼ ounce (7 g) white pepper
¼ ounce (7 g) ground ginger
¼ ounce (7 g) nutmeg
2 eggs
1 cup (236 ml) cream
29–32 mm hog casings

METHOD

1. Dice the pork into small, 1-inch (2.5 cm) cubes.

2. In a large bowl, mix all of the ingredients except for the eggs and cream together with your hands until they are equally distributed.

3. Grind the mixture two times through a grinder on a medium die.

4. After each run through the grinder, use your hands to mix the ingredients together and fully emulsify the loose sausage. (The mixture should be sticky and well combined and should stick to your hand when it's turned upside down.)

5. Using your hands, add the cream and eggs. Mix the ingredients thoroughly, until the mixture becomes sticky and emulsified. (The sausage should stick to your hand when it's turned upside down.)

6. Add the loose sausage mixture to the stuffer; pack it down to remove all of the air pockets.

7. Stuff the sausage into the hog casings and twist links 3 to 1 pound (455 g). (Generally, each sausage should be 5 to 6 inches [13 to 15 cm] long.)

8. Lightly poke each sausage link with a poking tool 3 or 4 times.

9. Put the twisted links in the refrigerator, uncovered, and chill overnight to dry out the casings.

10. Snip the sausages at the seams to separate them into links.

NOTE

We also used this recipe for a cooking competition, but substituted smoked duck for pork. These Smoked Duck Bratwursts were amazing! Maybe one of the best wurst ever.

Hot Brat[wurst]

YIELD: 5 POUNDS (2.27 KG)/15 • LINKS DIE: 3/16 (MEDIUM)

It was summertime of 2012 when we realized that people had become familiar with our sausages and our products. "Maybe y'all ought to try doing something kind of fun," they implored, "like something spicy!" Talk about fun: a hot bratwurst. Because Chris is a weenie when it comes to spicy food, we waited until he was sunbathing by the pool to play around with spicing things up in the sausage department. Fortunately, the addition of cayenne pepper and red pepper flakes added just enough heat to jazz up our sausage selection, but not so much as to take Chris out. "I mean I can eat it," he says, "I'm just sweating the whole time I do." We'd call that a success.

5 pounds (2.27 kg) pork

1¾ ounces (50 g) salt

¼ ounce (7 g) white pepper

¼ ounce (7 g) ground ginger

¼ ounce (7 g) nutmeg

Pinch of cayenne

½ ounce (14 g) red pepper flakes

2 eggs

1 cup (235 ml) cream

29–32 mm hog casings

METHOD

1. Dice the pork into small, 1-inch (2.5 cm) cubes.

2. In a large bowl, mix all of the ingredients except for the eggs and cream together with your hands until they are equally distributed.

3. Grind the mixture two times through a grinder on a medium die.

4. After each run through the grinder, use your hands to mix the ingredients together and fully emulsify the loose sausage.

5. After the second grind, add the cream and eggs. Mix the ingredients very thoroughly, until the mixture becomes sticky and emulsified. (The sausage should stick to your hand when it's turned upside down.)

6. Add the loose sausage mixture to the stuffer; pack it down to remove all of the air pockets.

7. Stuff the sausage into the hog casings and twist links 3 to 1 pound (455 g). (Generally, each sausage should be 5 to 6 inches [13 to 15 cm] long.)

8. Lightly poke each sausage link with a poking tool 3 or 4 times.

9. Put the twisted links in the refrigerator, uncovered, and chill overnight to dry out the casings.

10. Snip the sausage at the seams to separate them into links.

Winterwurst

YIELD: 5 POUNDS (2.27 KG)/15 • LINKS DIE: 3/16 (MEDIUM)

When the holidays roll around, everyone at the shop gets in the spirit. Chris's grandmother spends almost a whole day decking our halls with boughs of holly, Nashville gets transported back in time with our yearly revival of the traditional holiday Spiced Round, and we subsequently find ourselves longing for those spicy-sweet flavors in all of our December food. Cue the Winterwurst. In an effort to create a sausage that sings of the season, this Porter Road Butcher original variation is spiced with clove and allspice, giving it those familiar flavors that evoke Christmas so clearly.

5 pounds (2.27 kg) pork
1½ ounces (42 g) salt
½ ounce (15 g) black pepper
⅓ ounce (9 g) coriander
¼ ounce (7 g) clove
¾ ounce (21 g) fresh oregano
¾ ounce (21 g) fresh parsley
¼ ounce (7 g) allspice
29–32 mm hog casings

METHOD

1. Dice the pork into small, 1-inch (2.5 cm) cubes.

2. In a large bowl, mix all of the ingredients together with your hands until they are equally distributed.

3. Grind the mixture two times through a grinder on a medium die.

4. After each run through the grinder, use your hands to mix the ingredients together and fully emulsify the loose sausage. (The mixture should be sticky and well combined and should stick to your hand when it's turned upside down.)

5. Add the loose sausage mixture to the stuffer; pack it down to remove all of the air pockets.

6. Stuff the sausage into the hog casings and twist links 3 to 1 pound (455 g). (Generally, each sausage should be 5 to 6 inches [13 to 15 cm] long.)

7. Lightly poke each sausage link with a poking tool 3 or 4 times.

8. Put the twisted links in the refrigerator, uncovered, and chill overnight to dry out the casings.

9. Snip the sausages at the seams to separate them into links.

Currywurst

YIELD: 5 POUNDS (2.27 KG)/15 • LINKS DIE: 3/16 (MEDIUM)

Created more than 100 years ago, Currywurst is an iconic food of German pop culture, and it is still served to this day as a favorite German street food. The dish is unapologetically uncomplicated, and it consists of just three main ingredients: a steamed and/or fried pork sausage and some variation of ketchup, which is mixed with curry powder. Our Currywurst is quite a bit different from the German street food sweetheart, because we mix garam masala into the pork and leave any sort of saucy tomatoes out of the equation. This Currywurst sausage has a beautiful balance of sweet and savory, and it tastes great straight off of the grill or out of the oven.

5 pounds (2.27 kg) pork
1¾ ounces (50 g) salt
¼ ounce (7 g) white pepper
¼ ounce (7 g) ground ginger
¼ ounce (7 g) ground nutmeg
⅓ ounce (9 g) garam masala
2 eggs
1 cup (235 ml) cream
29–32 mm hog casings

METHOD

1. Cut the pork into small, 1-inch (2.5 cm) cubes.
2. In a large bowl, mix all of the ingredients except for the eggs and cream with your hands until they are equally distributed.
3. Grind the mixture two times through a grinder on a medium die.
4. After each run through the grinder, use your hands to mix the ingredients together and fully emulsify the loose sausage. (The mixture should be sticky and well combined and should stick to your hand when it's turned upside down.)
5. Using your hands, add the cream and eggs. Mix the ingredients very thoroughly, until the mixture becomes sticky and emulsified; the sausage should stick to your hand when it's turned upside down.
6. Add the loose sausage mixture to the stuffer; pack it down to remove all of the air pockets.
7. Stuff the sausage into the hog casings and twist links 3 to 1 pound (455 g). (Generally, each sausage should be 5 to 6 inches [13 to 15 cm] long.)
8. Lightly poke each sausage link with a poking tool 3 or 4 times.
9. Put the twisted links in the refrigerator, uncovered, and chill overnight to dry out the casings.
10. Snip the sausage at the seams to separate them into links.

Knackwursts

YIELD: 4 POUNDS (1.8 KG)/12 • LINKS DIE: 3/16 (MEDIUM)

Admittedly, Knackwursts are not familiar sausages to customers who frequent our shop because veal is something that we (almost) never ever carry. But when Hatcher Family Dairy Farm—the folks who provide us with our delicious local milk—had a dairy cow that calved a male, they knew what to do with him. They decided to finish the male calf on both pasture and on his mother's milk, the most humane way possible, and then sell him to us. So when we got this very special kind of meat into our shop, we knew we had to seize the opportunity to do something great and traditional: Knackwursts.

4 pounds (1.8 kg) veal
⅝ ounce (18 g) salt
⅛ ounce (4 g) pink salt
¼ ounce (7 g) black pepper
Pinch of nutmeg
⅛ ounce (4 g) paprika
Pinch of coriander
Pinch of allspice
1 ounce (28 g) milk powder
29–32 mm hog casings

METHOD

1. Cut the veal into small, 1-inch (2.5 cm) cubes.

2. In a large bowl, mix all of the ingredients together with your hands until they are equally distributed.

3. Grind the mixture two times through a grinder on a medium die.

4. After each run through the grinder, use your hands to mix the ingredients together and fully emulsify the loose sausage. (The sausage should stick to your hand when it is turned upside down.)

5. Add the loose sausage mixture to the stuffer; pack it down to remove all of the air pockets.

6. Stuff the sausage into the hog casings and twist links 3 to 1 pound (455 g). (Generally, each sausage should be 5 to 6 inches [13 to 15 cm] long.)

7. Lightly poke each sausage link with a poking tool 3 or 4 times.

8. Put the twisted links in the refrigerator, uncovered, and chill overnight to dry out the casings.

9. Snip the sausages at the seams to separate them into links.

Bacon Jalapeño Bratwurst

YIELD: 5 POUNDS (2.27 KG)15 • LINKS DIE: 3/16 (MEDIUM)

When our friends from Old School Farm (OSF) showed up at our shop in the summer of 2014 with mountains of jalapeños, we came up with a fantastic idea that would use both our unsightly bacon ends and their excess spicy pepper crop. Always up for some good old-fashioned bartering, we explained our plan to OSF. We got to take every last jalapeño off of their hands at little to no cost, and in exchange they received Bacon Jalapeño Bratwursts and Porter Road Butcher hamburgers for their Friday Night Farm Dances. So they were able to enjoy the fruits of their bounty after all! We all shook hands, and the deal was done. Bacon Jalapeño Bratwursts have been a fan favorite ever since.

3.75 pounds (1.7 kg) pork
1.25 pounds (567 g) bacon
1½ ounces (43 g) salt
¼ ounce (7 g) white pepper
¼ ounce (7 g) powdered ginger
¼ ounce (7 g) ground nutmeg
1¾ ounces (50 g) jalapeños
1 cup (235 ml) cream
2 eggs
2 ounces (55 g) scallions, sliced
29–32 mm hog casings

METHOD

1. Dice the pork and bacon into small, 1-inch (2.5 cm) cubes.
2. In a large bowl, mix all of the ingredients together, except for the eggs, cream, and scallions, until they are equally distributed.
3. Grind the mixture two times through a grinder on a medium die.
4. After each run through the grinder, use your hands to mix the ingredients together and fully emulsify the loose sausage.
5. Following the second grind, use your hands to add the cream, eggs, and scallions. Mix the ingredients thoroughly, until the mixture becomes sticky and emulsified. (The sausage should stick to your hand when it's turned upside down.)
6. Stuff the sausage into the hog casings and twist links 3 to 1 pound (455 g). (Generally, each sausage should be 5 to 6 inches [13 to 15 cm] long.)
7. Lightly poke each sausage link with a poking tool 3 or 4 times.
8. Put the twisted links in the refrigerator, uncovered, and chill overnight to dry out the casings.
9. Snip the sausages at the seams to separate them into links.

South African Boerewors

YIELD: 4 POUNDS (1.8 KG)/1 SPIRAL LINK DIE: 3/16 (MEDIUM)

Sausage is one of those foods that for many people is extremely nostalgic. Because it is often born as the love child of leftover yet traditional scraps of food, sausage holds memories and stories. With so many fond flavors in one bite, this makes sausage into a crown jewel of flavor. This recipe for Boerewors came to us from a customer who had recently relocated to Nashville from South Africa and was desperate for a taste of home—for a taste of tradition. Her butcher in South Africa actually sent her the recipe, and she brought it to us, hopeful that we would be able to grant her wish. We did, and we loved it. And so did she.

3 pounds (1.4 kg) beef
1 pound (455 g) pork fat
1¾ ounces (50 g) salt
⅛ ounce (4 g) black pepper
1⅛ ounces (32 g) coriander
Pinch of ground cloves
Pinch of nutmeg
29–32 mm hog casings

METHOD

1. In a large bowl, mix all of the ingredients together with your hands until they are evenly distributed.

2. Grind the mixture two times through a grinder on a medium die.

3. Using your hands, mix the ingredients again thoroughly until they become sticky and emulsified. (The sausage should stick to your hand when it's turned upside down.)

4. Add the loose sausage mixture to the stuffer; pack it down to remove all of the air pockets.

5. Stuff the sausage into the hog casings and do not twist. Instead, spiral it into one tight coil.

6. Lightly poke the entire spiral roughly every 3 inches (7.5 cm), starting from the center of the spiral and working all the way to the end.

7. Put the sausage spiral into the refrigerator, uncovered, and chill overnight to dry out the casings.

THE LITTLE LAMBS

Because lambs are significantly smaller animals than hogs, and because pork is usually the main protein that we use for making sausages, when it comes to lamb sausage, our repertoire of original lamb sausage recipes is also significantly smaller. The four recipes that we have listed here are all very different, but each one is incredibly flavorful and robust. Because people can be fearful of the gamier, sweeter, and overall stronger flavor of lamb in comparison to the well-known and familiar pork flavor, that fear can then prevent them from trying lamb sausages, but we're here to tell you that it shouldn't.

The sweet flavor of lamb, mixed with the compilation of incredibly robust ingredients used here, make these sausages true standouts—in the best meaning of the word.

Lamb Merguez

YIELD: 5 POUNDS (2.27 KG)/15 • LINKS DIE: 3/16 (MEDIUM)

Lamb Merguez is a traditional North African sausage that is heavily seasoned, oftentimes spicy, and always rich in flavor. These sausages are particularly popular in Morocco, and they are commonly served with traditional fare such as couscous, white beans, or vegetables. With such a rich and hearty flavor profile, however, Merguez is equally delicious served all by itself; it can win over the audience without much support from the chorus line. Absent in our Merguez is the traditional North African spice, harissa, which makes our version milder in heat, but still full in flavor. If you're a heat lover, however, feel free to bring on the harissa in your recipe!

5 pounds (2.27 kg) lamb
1½ ounces (43 g) salt
¼ ounce (7 g) black pepper
⅓ ounce (9 g) red pepper flakes
½ ounce (14 g) sweet paprika
¼ ounce (7 g) cumin
⅝ ounce (18 g) garlic
½ ounce (14 g) fresh oregano
Pinch of fresh thyme
⅝ ounce (18 g) scallions
29–32 mm hog casings

METHOD

1. In a large bowl, mix all of the ingredients together with your hands until they are equally distributed.
2. Grind the mixture two times through a grinder on a medium die.
3. Using your hands, mix the ingredients again thoroughly until the mixture becomes sticky and emulsified. (The sausage should stick to your hand when it's turned upside down.)
4. Add the loose sausage mixture to a stuffer; pack it down to remove all of the air pockets.
5. Stuff the sausage into the hog casings and twist links 3 to 1 pound (455 g). (Generally, each sausage should be 5 to 6 inches [13 to 15 cm] long.)
6. Lightly poke each sausage link with a poking tool 3 or 4 times.
7. Put the twisted links in the refrigerator, uncovered, and chill overnight to dry out the casings.
8. Snip the sausages at the seams to separate them into links.

Lamb Diablo

YIELD: 5 POUNDS (2.27 KG)/15 • LINKS DIE: 3/16 (MEDIUM)

It was a Wednesday afternoon in October when we had broken down two lambs and were left with plenty of meat that was ready to be ground, stuffed, and twisted into Lamb Merguez sausage links . . . until we realized we were short on ingredients. With the absence of oregano, Merguez sausage was taken off the table, but time was working against us as we brainstormed ideas for a new lamb sausage. James proposed a spicy lamb sausage—to excite the taste buds of those who love the heat—and his idea paid off. After we sold out of the first batch, people began inquiring for more, and soon Lamb Diablo became a steadfast staple sausage.

5 pounds (2.27 kg) lamb, cut into 1-inch (2.5 cm) cubes

1¾ ounces (50 g) salt

⅓ ounce (10 g) black pepper

1 ounce (28 g) garlic

13 ounces (364 g) chopped onion

½ cup (120 g) sambal (chili paste)

29–32 mm hog casings

METHOD

1. In a large bowl, mix all of the ingredients together with your hands until they are equally distributed.
2. Grind the mixture two times through a grinder on a medium die.
3. Using your hands, mix the ingredients again thoroughly until the mixture becomes sticky and emulsified. (The sausage should stick to your hand when it's turned upside down.)
4. Add the loose sausage mixture to the stuffer; pack it down to remove all of the air pockets.
5. Stuff the sausage into the hog casings and twist links 3 to 1 pound (455 g). (Generally, each sausage should be 5 to 6 inches [13 to 15 cm] long.)
6. Lightly poke each sausage link with a poking tool 3 or 4 times.
7. Put the twisted links in the refrigerator, uncovered, and chill overnight to dry out the casings.
8. Snip the sausages at the seams to separate them into links.

Lamb Chumichurri

YIELD: 5 POUNDS (2.27 KG)/15 • LINKS DIE: 3/16 (MEDIUM)

Chimichurri is one of our favorite things. You could say we have an obsession with it. It's flavorful, fresh-tasting, and best of all, versatile. With fresh herbs as the foundation of this sauce, chimichurri works well on steak, would easily jazz up a side of sad-looking vegetables, and could even be used to make a quick and easy, light pasta sauce. The only thing we don't like about chimichurri is all the chopping. That's why putting it into a sausage makes so much sense. The grinder does all the chopping for you. This sausage is great on the grill and with a side of chimichurri.

5 pounds (2.27 kg) lamb
1½ ounces (43 g) salt
¼ ounce (7 g) black pepper
⅛ ounce (4 g) red pepper flakes
⅞ ounce (25 g) garlic
⅞ ounce (25 g) fresh oregano
1¾ ounces (50 g) fresh parsley
29–32 mm hog casings

METHOD

1. In a large bowl, mix all of the ingredients together with your hands until they are equally distributed.

2. Grind the mixture two times through a grinder on a medium die.

3. Using your hands, mix the ingredients again thoroughly until the mixture becomes sticky and emulsified. (The sausage should stick to your hand when it's turned upside down.)

4. Add the loose sausage mixture to the stuffer; pack it down to remove all of the air pockets.

5. Stuff the sausage into the hog casings and twist links 3 to 1 pound (455 g). (Generally, each sausage should be 5 to 6 inches [13 to 15 cm] long.)

6. Lightly poke each sausage link with a poking tool 3 or 4 times.

7. Put the twisted links in the refrigerator, uncovered, and chill overnight to dry out the casings.

8. Snip the sausages at the seams to separate them into links.

Lambdouille

YIELD: 5 POUNDS (2.27 KG)/15 • LINKS DIE: ⅜ (LARGE)

Lamb is harder to sell than other types of meat because it has a stronger, sweeter, and somewhat earthier flavor. We've come to find that people either love it or seriously do not. Once the main cuts like loin chops, rack of lamb, and leg of lamb have sold out, we either have to work hard to sell what's left or figure out what to do with the meat before it goes bad. Itching for something new to play around with and tired of the same ole Merguez that we often employ for lamb, the guys at the East Nashville shop came up with this smoky, lamb-centric version of the Louisiana classic Andouille, and we've got to say: it's delicious. The play-on-words certainly doesn't hurt, either.

5 pounds (2.27 g) lamb

1½ ounces (43 g) salt

Pinch of pink salt

Pinch of ground white pepper

⅓ ounce (9 g) cumin

1 ounce (28 g) ancho chile powder

Pinch of cayenne

¼ ounce (7 g) paprika

2 ounces (56 g) milk powder

¼ cup (60 ml) ice water

Pinch of sliced scallions

29–32 mm hog casings

METHOD

1. In a large bowl, mix all of the ingredients, except for the water and scallions, together with your hands until they are equally distributed.

2. Grind the mixture once a through grinder on a large die.

3. Using your hands, add the scallions and mix into the once-ground mixture. Once it is completely combined, run the mixture through the grinder one more time on the same medium die.

4. Add the ice water to the mixture and then use your hands to incorporate the water into ground sausage mix. Combine it thoroughly, until the mixture becomes sticky and emulsified.

5. Add the loose sausage mixture to the stuffer; pack it down to remove all of the air pockets.

6. Stuff the sausage into the hog casings and twist links 3 to 1 pound (455 g). (Generally, each sausage should be 5 to 6 inches [13 to 15 cm] long.) Do not poke.

7. Put the twisted links in the refrigerator, uncovered, and chill overnight to dry out the casings.

8. Smoke the sausages at 225°F (107°C) for 1 hour, or until the internal temperature is 150°F (65°C).

9. Cool the sausages completely and then snip them at the seams to separate them into links.

THE SMOKERS

Ah, the smokers. In today's modern and health-conscious age, smoking—and consequently people who smoke—are often frowned upon because of the damage done to their lungs and speedy deterioration of their health.

In the sausage world, however, smokers are coveted, glorified, and overall desirable and delicious. In the sausage world, "smokers" aren't classified as people who smoke; they are classified as sausages that are smoked by people.

In reality, any sausage in the whole entire world could be thrown on the smoker and given that extra layer of rich, woody, delicious flavor. For that matter, almost any consumable product could be afforded said opportunity, but the following three links are our go-tos when it comes to the smoker—meaning they are always smoked, and they are never served fresh. These sausages emerge from the clouds with slightly taught skin and beautiful char marks that get our mouths watering and our nostrils flaring.

Andouille

YIELD: 5 POUNDS (2.27 KG)/15 • LINKS DIE: ⅜ (LARGE)

Sure, we like to stick to tradition when it comes to food, but on the other hand, it can also be fun to step out, take the road less traveled, and try something new every now and again. Any Louisiana native will immediately notice one major difference in our Andouille: it's noticeably smaller in size as opposed to the horseshoe-shaped full pound (455 g) link they're used to back home. The flavors, however, do come closer to the classic Cajun link. Our Andouille can be used in a variety of ways to add some incredible smoke and richness to any dish.

5 pounds (2.27 kg) pork

1½ ounces (43 g) salt

¼ ounce (7 g) pink salt

Pinch of ground white pepper

¼ ounce (7 g) cumin

⅞ ounce (25 g) ancho chile powder

Pinch of cayenne

¼ ounce (7 g) paprika

2 ounces (57 g) milk powder

¼ cup (60 ml) ice water

Pinch of sliced scallions

29–32 mm hog casings

METHOD

1. In a large bowl, mix all of the ingredients, except for the water and scallions, together with your hands until they are equally distributed.

2. Grind the mixture once through a grinder on a large die.

3. Using your hands, add the scallions and mix them into the once-ground mixture. Once completely combined, grind the mixture through the grinder one more time on the same large die.

4. Add the ice water to the mixture and then use your hands to incorporate the water into the ground sausage mix. Combine it thoroughly, until the mixture becomes sticky and emulsified.

5. Add the loose sausage mixture to the stuffer; pack it down to remove all of the air pockets.

6. Stuff the sausage into the hog casings and twist links 3 to 1 pound (455 g). (Generally, each sausage should be 5 to 6 inches [13 to 15 cm] long. Do not poke.

7. Put the twisted links in the refrigerator, uncovered, and chill overnight to dry out the casings.

8. Smoke the sausages at 225°F (107°C) for 1 hour, or until the internal temperature is 150°F (65°C).

9. Cool the sausages completely and then snip them at the seams to separate them into links.

Summer Sausage

YIELD: 5 POUNDS (2.27 KG)/5 • LINKS DIE: 1/8 (SMALL)

The first time that we decided to make Summer Sausage just so happened to fall on a pretty big day of the year: Super Bowl Sunday, which, oddly enough, is not in the summer. Because we had to order special casings for this particular type of sausage, we chose to go all out in light of the event and ordered football-shaped casings, laces and all. When we stuffed and then smoked the sausages and they came out looking like footballs, we were sure they would sell out quickly, and we were right—despite the fact that one of our employees accidentally labeled them "Surper Bowl Sausages" in our case. This smoky sausage pairs well with cheese and crackers, plenty of good beer, and of course, football.

5 pounds (2.27 kg) beef
1 ounce (28 g) mustard
2 ounces (57 g) garlic
⅓ ounce (9 g) coriander
⅛ ounce (4 g) red pepper flakes
⅛ ounce (4 g) black pepper
2 42–45 mm large hog casings

METHOD

1. Dice the beef into small, 1-inch (2.5 cm) cubes.

2. In a large bowl, mix all of the ingredients together with your hands until they are equally distributed.

3. Grind the mixed ingredients four times through a grinder on a small die. Keep the mixture very cold during the grinding process; if the meat begins to lose its chill, return it to the refrigerator before continuing to grind.

4. Add the loose sausage mixture to the stuffer; pack it down to remove all of the air pockets.

5. Stuff the ground meat into a large hog casing and tie it off at the end. Twist into five 1-pound (455 g) links. Do not poke the links. The links should be around 12 inches (30.5 cm) in length.

6. Put the sausage in the fridge, uncovered, overnight to allow the sausage to set and the casings to dry out.

7. Smoke the sausages at 225°F (107°C) for 1½ to 2 hours.

8. Cool the sausages completely. Slice thinly and use as a topping for pizza or sandwich meat.

Porteroni

YIELD: 5 POUNDS (2.27 KG)/5 • LINKS DIE: 1 /8 (SMALL)

Porteroni is our version of a classic pepperoni, and it's pretty much as simple as that. Although pepperoni is traditionally cured meat, our Porteroni is semi-cured and then smoked, giving it a similar consistency to that of pepperoni and just as long of a shelf life. Pepperoni is usually made from a mixture of beef and pork—serving as a way to use up scraps of animals and turning it into one of our favorite pizza toppings—but for Porteroni we stick to purely beef. Try it on top of a pizza, as a filling for calzone, or even in an omelet! It brings a bold flavor to everything it touches.

5 pounds (2.27 kg) fatty beef

1 ounce (28 g) salt

½ ounce (14 g) pink salt

¾ ounce (21 g) sugar

½ ounce (14 g) red pepper flakes

½ ounce (14 g) hot paprika

½ ounce (14 g) sweet paprika

¼ ounce (7 g) cayenne

¾ ounce (21 g) fennel seed, toasted and ground

¾ ounce (21 g) garlic

2 42–45 mm large hog casings

METHOD

1. Dice the fatty beef into 1-inch (2.5 cm) cubes.

2. In a bowl, mix the salt and pink salt together to create a cure.

3. In a large bowl, toss the fatty beef in the salt mixture, covering each piece. Put the beef in the fridge and cure it for two days.

4. Remove the beef from the fridge and using your hands, mix it together with the remaining ingredients.

5. Grind the mixed ingredients four times through a grinder on a small die. Keep the mixture very cold during the grinding process; if the meat begins to lose its chill, return it to the refrigerator before continuing to grind.

6. Add the loose sausage mixture to the stuffer; pack it down to remove all of the air pockets.

7. Stuff the ground meat into a large hog casing and tie it off at the end. Twist it into five 1-pound (455 g) links. Do not poke the links. The links should be around 12 inches (30 cm) in length.

8. Put the sausage in the fridge, uncovered, overnight to allow the sausage to set and the casings to dry out.

9. Smoke the sausages at 225°F (107°C) for 1½ to 2 hours.

10. Allow the sausages to cool completely. Slice thinly and use as a topping for pizza or sandwich meat.

THE SOUTHERNERS

If you took a survey of the southern half of the United States, you would likely find a wide variation in culture across the board. You would notice a difference in the local accents, a difference in the traditional food, a difference in the favored music, and even a difference in the common entertainment, which would vary from city to city, and state to state. But if there's one thing that southerners all have in common, it's their pride for being just that: Southern.

As a butcher shop that was born in Tennessee, our Southern pride is no different than any other Southern soul's, and we display our pride through our food—sausage included. These sausages show that they are Southern through the ingredients they require and the memories they evoke.

Whether it's "Rocky Top" that's your anthem, "Georgia on my Mind" that brings you right back home, or "Sweet Home Alabama" that gets your toe a-tappin', any Southerner from any of our hot and humid states will feel a little more at home with the following recipes.

Louisiana Hot Links

YIELD: 5 POUNDS (2.27 KG)/15 • LINKS DIE: 3/16 (MEDIUM)

Back in Porter Road Butcher's early days, we noticed an influx of customers hailing from New Orleans who continually patronized our shop. Coming from a land where fresh sausages and local butchers weren't the same kind of novelty that ours was (and still is) in Nashville, they expected to find products in our case similar to those they would find in the meat markets from their homeland. And though we did have a mean Andouille to offer them, we received quite a few inquiries for spicy Louisiana links. So we obliged. Hey, it's always fun to have an excuse to experiment! We found the list of ingredients on a grocery store reconnaissance, and soon our New Orleans native customers left the shop with a giant smile on their faces and fire in their eyes and bellies.

5 pounds (2.27 kg) pork

1½ ounces (43 g) salt

¼ ounce (7 g) black pepper

⅛ ounce (4 g) cayenne pepper

½ ounce (14 g) red pepper flakes

⅞ ounce (25 g) hot paprika

¼ ounce (7 g) garlic powder

Pinch of allspice

Pinch of dried bay leaves

½ ounce (14 g) mustard seed

29–32 mm hog casings

METHOD

1. In a large bowl, mix all of the ingredients together with your hands until they are equally distributed.

2. Grind the mixture two times through a grinder on a medium die.

3. Using your hands, mix the ingredients again thoroughly until they become sticky and emulsified. (The sausage should stick to your hand when it's turned upside down.)

4. Add the loose sausage mixture to the stuffer; pack it down to remove all of the air pockets.

5. Stuff the sausage into the hog casings and twist links 3 to 1 pound (455 g). (Generally, each sausage should be 5 to 6 inches [13 to 15 cm] long.)

6. Lightly poke each sausage link with a poking tool 3 or 4 times.

7. Put the twisted links in the refrigerator, uncovered, and chill overnight to dry out the casings.

8. Snip the sausage at the seams to separate them into links.

Memphis Sausage

YIELD: 5 POUNDS (2.27 KG)/5 • LINKS DIE: 3/16 (MEDIUM)

Back in his college days, Chris Carter was known among his group of friends for being a whiz on the barbecue. He was skilled with cooking and grilling meat, and he and his friend's original barbecue rub was loved by all who were fortunate to have a taste. Many years later when said friend, Chris Hudgens, was hired on as one of Porter Road Butcher's first employees, Hudge immediately felt nostalgic to be working in the kitchen with his old barbecuing friend Carter, and even more so to be using that same BBQ rub in the shop. With the title of "sausage maker" handed to him after a few short months, Hudge couldn't hold in his longing for Memphis BBQ much longer, and thus decided to pay tribute to his hometown with a Memphis-style BBQ Sausage. This link is one of our bestsellers during the summer months. It's perfect for grilling and easily brings that big, bold, savory-sweet BBQ flavor to the party without all of the fuss.

5 pounds (2.27 kg) pork

⅓ ounce (9 g) fresh black pepper

⅓ ounce (9 g) white pepper

1½ ounces (43 g) salt

2½ ounces (71 g) brown sugar

¾ ounce (21 g) smoked paprika

¼ ounce (7 g) red pepper flakes

3⅓ ounces (94 g) scallions

¼ ounce (7 g) garlic

¼ ounce (7 g) ancho chile powder

1 ounce (30 ml) bourbon

1 ounce (28 g) mustard

½ ounce (14 g) honey

½ ounce (14 g) tomato paste

29–32 mm hog casings

METHOD

1. In a large bowl, add all of the ingredients except for the bourbon, mustard, honey, and tomato paste. Mix them together with your hands until they are equally distributed.

2. Grind the mixture two times through a grinder on a medium die.

3. Add the wet ingredients (bourbon, mustard, honey, and tomato paste) to the ground mixture and mix thoroughly, until the mixture becomes sticky and emulsified. (The sausage should stick to your hand when it's turned upside down.)

4. Add the loose sausage mixture to the stuffer; pack it down to remove all of the air pockets.

5. Stuff the sausage into the hog casings and twist links 3 to 1 pound (455 g). (Generally, each sausage should be 5 to 6 inches [13 to 15 cm] long.)

6. Put the twisted links in the refrigerator, uncovered, and chill overnight to dry out the casings.

7. Snip the sausage at the seams to separate them into links.

Boudin

YIELD: 4 POUNDS (1.8 KG)/12 • LINKS DIE: 3/16 (MEDIUM)

Similar to chorizo, Boudin is a sausage that can't firmly connect its name to one specific product or list of ingredients. The components that make up this sausage differ based upon the prefix or suffix that accompanies it, as well as the place of origin. Boudin noir, dark and red in appearance, is a "blood sausage" that actually necessitates pork blood in an effort to make the sausage rich, moist, and velvety in texture. Boudin blanc, on the other hand, eliminates blood from the equation and only uses white meat like chicken or other poultry. Our Boudin, unlike either of the formerly mentioned French-style Boudin sausages, has more Cajun tendencies, incorporating rice, pork liver, and hot sauce to bring out those beloved Louisiana flavors.

4 pounds (1.8 kg) pork

1 pound (455 g) pork liver

2 onions, roughly chopped

½ head celery, roughly chopped

½ red bell pepper, roughly chopped

10 cloves garlic, roughly chopped

¼ cup (60 ml) Worcestershire sauce

¾ cup (175 ml) hot sauce

3 bay leaves

1½ teaspoons gumbo file powder

1 tablespoon (5.3 g) cayenne pepper

½ cup (120 g) Creole mustard

8 cups (½ gallon, [1.9 L]) pork stock

4 cups (780 g) medium-grain rice

3⅓ ounces (100 g) scallions

1¼ ounces (35 g) fresh parsley

29–32 mm hog casings

METHOD

1. Separately cut the pork and pork liver into small, 1-inch (2.5 cm) cubes.

2. Over medium-high heat, brown the pork in a large stockpot. Once browned, add the onion, celery, bell pepper, and garlic and cook until translucent.

3. Add the cubed pork livers and sauté until browned.

4. Add the remaining ingredients, except for the rice, scallions, and parsley, and simmer over low heat for 4 hours.

5. Using a colander or large strainer, strain the meat mixture from the cooking liquid. Be sure to reserve the cooking liquid—do not throw it out!

6. Set the mixture aside and cool it completely in the refrigerator overnight.

7. Meanwhile, bring the cooking liquid to a boil in a large pot with a lid. Add the rice to the liquid and reduce the heat to low. Replace the lid on the pot and cook the rice for 15 to 20 minutes, or according to the package instructions. Strain the excess cooking liquid (if any) and discard. Set aside the rice and let it cool completely overnight.

8. In the morning, add the rice to a large bowl and set it below the mouth of the grinder. Grind the cooled meat mixture once on a medium die, allowing it to fall into the bowl with the rice.

9. Using your hands, mix the rice and ground meat together until they are integrated. Finally, mix in the parsley and scallions with your hands until evenly distributed.

10. Add the loose sausage mixture to the stuffer; pack it down to remove all of the air pockets.

11. Stuff the sausage into the hog casings and twist links 3 to 1 pound (455 g). (Generally, each sausage should be 5 to 6 inches [13 to 15 cm] long.)

12. Lightly poke each sausage link 3 or 4 times with a poking tool.

13. Put the twisted links in the refrigerator, uncovered, and chill overnight to dry out the casings.

14. Snip the sausages at the seams to separate them into links.

Tennessee Mortadella

YIELD: 10 POUNDS (4.5 KG)/1 LOGDIE: 1/8 (SMALL)

One reason we love Tennessee Mortadella is because of the juxtaposition of cultures that makes our brains spin as we try to make sense of it. Mortadella is the Italian grandfather of what we know in America as that uniform, circular, and bubblegum pink lunchmeat called "baloney." Originating in Bologna, Italy, Mortadella shares a skeleton with bologna, but it has undergone far less cosmetic-corrective surgery. Mortadella is known for ingredients like chunks of fat, bright green pistachios, or even whole, unground spices that are suspended throughout the cylindrical meat, giving it beautiful texture and color. The lunchmeat now associated with the American south, on the other hand, is so overly processed, it looks perfectly smooth and lacks any inconsistencies. For this Tennessee-skewed version of Italian Mortadella, we crossed back over the pond to add some Southern flair: Tennessee whiskey and chunks of jowl bacon. Yeehaw!

10 pounds (4.5 kg) fatty beef

2 ounces (57 g) salt

1 ounce (28 g) pink salt

1⅛ ounces (32 g) black pepper

½ ounce (14 g) white pepper

½ ounce (14 g) mustard powder

½ ounce (14 g) garlic

12.8 ounces (363 ml) Tennessee whiskey

1½ pounds (680 ml) jowl bacon, unsliced

4.84 x 27-inch (12.3 x 68.5 cm) synthetic, fibrous casing

METHOD

1. Dice the fatty beef into 1-inch (2.5 cm) cubes.

2. Mix the salts together to create a cure.

3. In a large bowl, toss the fatty beef in the salt mixture, covering each piece. Put the beef in the fridge and let it cure for two days.

4. Remove the beef from the fridge and using your hands, mix it together with the remaining ingredients, except for the whiskey and jowl bacon.

5. Grind the mixed ingredients four times through a grinder on a small die. Keep the mixture very cold during the grinding process; if the meat begins to lose its chill, return it to the refrigerator before continuing to grind.

6. Before grinding the meat for the fourth time, add the whiskey to it, and incorporate it with your hands. Grind it through a small die for the fourth time, allowing the whiskey to aid in emulsifying the meat.

7. Dice the jowl bacon into roughly 1-inch (2.5 cm) cubes. Using your hands, incorporate it into the ground meat until it is evenly distributed. (This will allow large hunks of bacon to appear when the meat is later sliced, adding texture and visual interest.)

8. Using the largest sausage horn available, stuff the ground meat into a synthetic mortadella (or bologna) casing and tie it off at the end.

9. Create a water bath big enough to submerge the entire mortadella roll, and bring the water temperature up to 150°F (65°C). Note: A circulator is a tool that helps maintain the temperature of the water and is vital for this style of cooking.

Cook the mortadella for 6 hours, or until the internal temperature reaches 150°F (65°C). Or fill a slow cooker full of water and set it to the highest setting. Submerge the mortadella in the water, taking care to tie the ends tightly to prevent water from seeping inside. After 2 hours, insert a thermometer into the center of the mortadella. Continue checking the mortadella every hour, until the internal temperature reaches 150°F (65°C). Remove it from the water and put it directly into an ice bath (a large bowl of ice water) to stop the cooking process.

10. Allow the mortadella to cool completely before removing the casing and/or slicing.

Nashville Hot Chicken Sausage

YIELD: 5 POUNDS (2.27 KG)/15 • LINKS DIE: 3/16 (MEDIUM)

Nashville has become somewhat of a food festival mecca over the past decade or so, but no food festival holds a candle to the East Nashville Hot Chicken Festival, which takes place every year on the Fourth of July. In preparation for our first ever Hot Chicken Festival back in 2012, we created this sausage to rival our "real" hot chicken competitors, such as Prince's, Hattie B's, and Bolton's. Even though we had beer on hand for the duration of the festival, nothing could quite tame our taste buds after feasting on a few of these fiery sausages. Word to the wise: beer is horrible for neutralizing a spicy mouth. Drinking milk or eating a piece of white bread is the most effective way to go.

4½ pounds (2 kg) boneless, skinless chicken thighs, quartered

½ pound (227 g) butter, ½-inch (1.3 cm) dice, frozen

1½ ounces (43 g) salt

¼ ounce (7 g) freshly ground black pepper

⅛ ounce (4 g) cayenne pepper

½ ounce (14 g) red pepper flakes

⅞ ounce (25 g) hot paprika

¼ ounce (7 g) garlic powder

Pinch of allspice

Pinch of dried bay leaves

½ ounce (14 g) mustard seed

29–32 mm hog casings

METHOD

1. Cut the chicken into small, 1-inch (2.5 cm) cubes.

2. Separately, cut the butter into roughly 1-inch (2.5 cm) cubes. Keep both the chicken and the butter very cold.

3. In a large bowl, mix all of the ingredients together with your hands until they are equally distributed.

4. Grind the mixture two times through a grinder on a medium die.

5. Using your hands, mix the ingredients again, very thoroughly, until it becomes sticky and emulsified. (The sausage should stick to your hand when it's turned upside down.)

6. Add the loose sausage mixture to the stuffer; pack it down to remove all of the air pockets.

7. Stuff the sausage into the hog casings and twist links 3 to 1 pound (455 g). (Generally, each sausage should be 5 to 6 inches [13 to 15 cm] long.)

8. Put the twisted links in the refrigerator, uncovered, and chill overnight to dry out the casings.

9. Snip the sausages at the seams to separate them into links.

10. Do not poke the sausages. Smoke the sausages at 225°F (107°C) for 1 hour, or until an internal temperature of 165°F (74°C).

THE NOT-QUITE-SAUSAGE

Most definitions qualify sausage as ground meat mixed with spices, and then stuffed into some sort of cylindrical casing, but the qualifications for being both stuffed and cylindrical need not always apply. Pâté, chilled and spreadable meats often made from animal offal and fat, might not be the first thing that comes to mind at the mention of sausage, but at their foundation fit all of the truly necessary requirements. Pâté was born as a way of using what would otherwise be discarded meat; it necessitates fat as an ingredient; and vegetables, spices, and herbs are usually mixed in to add flavor and flair.

The difference? Pâté does not come in a casing. Pâté is cooked in a terrine, in a water bath, at a lower heat, and is then pressed and chilled before being eaten. Pâté is not usually grilled, sautéed, or broiled; but simply spread on crackers or toast and enjoyed with cheese. So while pâté still lives in the brotherhood of sausage, in reality the two are closer to cousins than first-of-kin.

Tennessee Pâté

YIELD: 5 POUNDS (2.27 KG)2 PÂTÉ • LOAVES DIE: 3/16 (MEDIUM)

The not-quite-sausages we've selected for this book go in descending order of boldness to ease in any of you pâté rookies slowly. We like to call our Tennessee Pâté, "pâté for beginners," because it contains no liver at all, but it still introduces the flavor, look, and consistency of a traditional pâté. Lacking that iron-y, and what some people consider to be undesirable flavor, we think this Southern version of the French favorite is pretty awesome.

5 pounds (2.27 kg) pork

¼ cup (75 g) salt

¼ ounce (7 g) black pepper

⅜ ounce (11 g) pink salt

¼ ounce (7 g) Pâté Spice (see recipe below)

2 ounces (57 g) fresh parsley

Pinch of fresh thyme

1¾ ounces (50 g) garlic

5¼ ounces (149 g) chopped onion

¼ cup (31 g) flour

4 eggs

1 cup (235 ml) cream

½ cup (118 ml) Tennessee whiskey, such as Jack Daniels

METHOD

1. Dice the pork into small, 1-inch (2.5 cm) cubes.

2. Mix all of the ingredients together, except for the eggs, cream, and whiskey.

3. Put the pork and spice mixture into the freezer until they are very cold, about 30 minutes.

4. Once the pork and spice mixture is thoroughly chilled, grind the pork mixture two times through a grinder on a medium die.

5. Add the eggs, cream, and whiskey, and mix everything together thoroughly with your hands.

6. Line a pâté terrine with oven-safe plastic wrap (available at most restaurant supply stores: try Darnell Wrap), leaving at least 6 inches (15 cm) of excess plastic wrap on all four sides. To receive a finished

PÂTÉ SPICE

Before you start, all three of our pâté recipes call for "Pâté Spice," which is a mixture of spices that we always keep on hand.

¼ ounce (7 g) ground cloves

¼ ounce (7 g) ground nutmeg

¼ ounce (7 g) ground ginger

¼ ounce (7 g) ground coriander

⅜ ounce (11 g) ground cinnamon

Pinch of white pepper

METHOD

In a small bowl, combine all of the ingredients. Store in a container with a lid in a cool, dry place at room temperature. Bon appétit!

product that looks beautiful and clean, first fill your plastic-wrapped terrine with water and use the weight of the water to press the plastic wrap to the edges of the terrine. The bottom and the edges should be smooth, with as few wrinkles as possible. Pour out the water.

7. Now press the meat mixture into the terrine. Note: It can be helpful to hit the bottom of the terrine on the counter or floor, being mindful to not hit it too hard that it breaks or cracks, which will help pack the meat into the terrine.

8. Once the terrine is filled and the meat packed down, use your hands to smooth out the top, again creating an even layer. Then cover the top of the meat with the excess plastic wrap and fold the edges of the wrap in, around the other sides of the loaf.

9. Put the terrine into a larger, ovenproof vessel (such as a Dutch oven or deep casserole dish—something that is deep enough so that the terrine does not peek out over the top), and fill the vessel with water to create a water bath. The water level should almost reach the top edge of the terrine, but the top should still be dry and open to the heat of the oven.

10. Cook at 325°F (170°C) degrees for 1½ hours, or until the internal temperature reaches 150°F (65°C).

11. Carefully remove the water bath and terrine from the oven together. Then carefully remove the terrine from the water bath and discard the water.

12. Using bricks or other heavy objects, press the terrine at room temperature for 1 hour.

13. Finally, move the terrine to the refrigerator and continue to press it overnight.

Country Pâté

YIELD: 5 POUNDS (2.27 KG)/2 PÂTÉ LOAVES DIE: 3/16 (MEDIUM)

You're getting there, you fearless pâté pioneer, you. You're getting close to "the real thing." Our Country Pâté has a liver-to-meat ratio of only 1:4, meaning the presence of liver is far inferior to that of the meat, thus this pâté has inserted itself as the middleman between a pâté pupil and a pâté purist. If you liked the Tennessee Pâté and you're ready to take your taste buds to the next level, this recipe will slowly introduce the flavor of pork liver to your palate. Said to be the strongest in flavor out of commonly consumed animal liver, pork liver isn't something that many people are comfortable diving right into. So, good for you for taking the first step! We know you're going to love it.

- 1 pound (455 g) pork liver
- 1 small onion, chopped
- ½ cup (120 ml) whiskey
- 4 pounds (1.8 kg) pork
- ¼ cup (75 g) salt
- 2 teaspoons pink salt
- 2 tablespoons (13 g) black pepper
- 2 tablespoons (14 g) Pâté Spice (see page 94)
- 2 tablespoons (5 g) fresh thyme
- 6 cloves garlic
- 2 tablespoons (8 g) fresh parsley
- 2 tablespoons (15 g) flour
- ½ cup (120 ml) cream
- 4 eggs

METHOD

1. In a sauté pan over very high heat, quickly sear the liver until brown. Note: Do not cook the liver. Only sear it on high heat. If the liver is cooked for a long period of time, it will take on an undesirable, grainy consistency instead of its traditional smooth mouth feel.

2. Add the onion and cook it until it's translucent.

3. Being mindful of the flame, deglaze the pan with the whiskey.

4. Put the mixture in the freezer to cool, about 30 minutes.

5. Remove it from the freezer and add all of the remaining ingredients, except for the flour, cream, and eggs. Using your hands, combine the mixture thoroughly.

6. Add the flour, cream, and eggs and thoroughly combine with your hands.

7. Using a medium die, run the mixture through a grinder twice, using your hands to further emulsify and combine the mixture after each grinder run.

8. Line a pâté terrine with oven-safe plastic wrap (available at most restaurant supply stores: try Darnell Wrap), leaving at least 6 inches (15 cm) of excess plastic wrap on all four sides. To receive a finished product that looks beautiful and clean, fill a plastic-wrapped terrine with water and use the weight of the water to press the plastic wrap to the edges of the terrine. The bottom and the edges should be smooth, with as few wrinkles as possible. Pour out the water.

9. Press the meat mixture into the terrine. Note: It can be helpful to hit the bottom of the terrine on the counter or floor, being mindful to not hit it too hard that you break or crack it, which will help pack the meat into the terrine.

10. Once the terrine is filled and the meat is packed down, use your hands to smooth out the top, again creating an even layer. Then cover the top of the meat with the excess plastic wrap and fold the edges of the wrap in, around the other sides of the loaf.

11. Once the meat is sealed in the plastic wrap, put the terrine into a larger, ovenproof vessel (like a Dutch oven or a deep casserole dish—something that is deep enough so that the terrine does not peek out over the top), and fill the vessel with water to create a water bath. The water level should almost reach the top edge of the terrine, but the top should still be dry and open to the heat of the oven.

12. Cook at 325°F (163°C) for 1½ hours, or until an internal temperature of 150°F (65°C).

13. Carefully remove the water bath and terrine from the oven together. Then carefully remove the terrine from the water bath and discard the water.

14. Using bricks or other heavy objects, press the terrine at room temperature for 1 hour.

15. Finally, refrigerate the terrine and continue to press it overnight.

Pork Liver and Bacon Pâté

YIELD: 5 POUNDS (2.27 KG)/2 PÂTÉ LOAVES DIE: 1/8 (SMALL)

Liver has a rich, iron-y taste that should be appreciated and celebrated rather than feared and avoided. The depth of flavor from this pork liver and bacon pâté is something to behold and love—plus, there's bacon in it! Nobody can be afraid of bacon. The creamy, smooth texture of the pâté makes it feel like butter as it melts onto your tongue, leaving a sweet pork and smoky bacon taste in its wake. Pork Liver and Bacon Pâté pairs perfectly with something simple like a cracker or good piece of toast. A dollop of fig jam or a smear of mustard is also sure to make your taste buds happy.

4 pounds (1.8 kg) pork liver

1 pound (455 g) bacon ends

½ pound (228 g) pork back fat

¼ cup (75 g) salt

2 teaspoons pink salt

2 tablespoons (13 g) black pepper

2 tablespoons (14 g) Pâté Spice (see page 94)

2 tablespoons (8 g) fresh parsley

2 tablespoons (5 g) fresh thyme

1 medium onion, roughly chopped

6 cloves garlic

1 cup (235 ml) whiskey

2 tablespoons (15 g) flour

½ cup (118 ml) cream

4 eggs

METHOD

1. Separately, cut the liver, bacon, and back fat into small, 1-inch (2.5 cm) pieces.

2. Using your hands, mix the liver, back fat, spices, and herbs thoroughly, and then place in the freezer to cool.

3. Meanwhile, in a sauté pan over medium-high heat, cook the bacon until golden brown.

4. Add the onion and garlic to the pan with the bacon, and cook until it is translucent.

5. Being mindful of the flames, carefully deglaze the pan with the whiskey.

6. Add the bacon-and-onion mixture to the liver mixture from freezer. Mix well.

7. Return the mixture to the freezer and allow it to cool completely, about 30 minutes.

8. Once the mixture has cooled, grind it four times on a small die.

9. Using your hands, mix in the flour, cream, and eggs until thoroughly combined and incorporated.

10. Line a pâté terrine with oven-safe plastic wrap (available at most restaurant supply stores: try Darnell Wrap), leaving at least 6 inches (15 cm) of excess plastic wrap on all four sides. To receive a finished product that looks beautiful and clean, fill a plastic-wrapped terrine with water and use the weight of the water to press the plastic wrap

to the edges of the terrine. The bottom and the edges should be smooth, with as few wrinkles as possible. Pour out the water.

11. Press the meat mixture into the terrine. Note: It can be helpful to hit the bottom of the terrine on the counter or floor, being mindful to not hit it too hard that it breaks or cracks. This will help pack the meat into the terrine.

12. Once the terrine is filled and the meat packed down, use your hands to smooth out the top, again creating an even layer. Then cover the top of the meat with the excess plastic wrap and fold the edges of the wrap in, around the other sides of the loaf.

13. Once the meat is sealed in the plastic wrap, put the terrine into a larger, ovenproof vessel (like a Dutch oven or a deep casserole dish—something that is deep enough so that the terrine does not peek out over the top), and fill the vessel with water to create a water bath. The water level should almost reach the top edge of the terrine, but the top should still be dry and open to the heat of the oven.

14. Cook at 325°F (170°C) degrees for 1½ hours, or until an internal temperature of 150°F (66°C).

15. Carefully remove the water bath and terrine from the oven together. Then carefully remove the terrine from the water bath and discard the water.

16. Using bricks or other heavy objects, press the terrine at room temperature for 1 hour.

17. Finally, move it to the refrigerator and continue to press it overnight.

CHAPTER 3

Twist

You've ground, you've stuffed, you've twisted, and you've worked so intently to make something that's truly delicious and one of a kind. Now it's time to put another twist on the masterpiece you just created. Because, if we're being honest with one another, the hard part is over. There's no more weighing out of ingredients, no more mixing things over and over again with your hands, and most importantly, no more being frustrated with the casing when you find a hole or it inevitably breaks. It's time to call up some friends, invite them over for dinner, and tell them to bring a bottle of wine or whiskey. The following recipes are sure to show off the true splendor of your homemade sausage. They're generally easy to prepare, simple, and delicious, too. Enjoy!

The Best Breakfast Sausage Biscuit

YIELD: 12 SANDWICHES

This sausage biscuit is one we sell for breakfast at our West Nashville shop six days a week through the drive-through window, and it is consistently one of our customers' favorites. The sausage is filled with fresh ingredients and robust spices; the biscuits come out of the oven golden-crisp on top and warm and fluffy in the middle; and the drizzle of local honey acts like the glue that holds everything together: no slipping and sliding around, plus an extra dose of sweetness to balance the savory sausage and biscuit. Oftentimes we'll add a fried egg or some local Cheddar cheese on top, but the good simplicity of a biscuit, sausage, and drizzle of honey does just the trick for us in the early morning. Who are we kidding? It does the trick for us any time of the day.

FOR THE BISCUITS

¼ pound (115 g) cold butter, plus extra melted for brushing

4 cups (480 g) unbleached all-purpose flour

1 tablespoon (14 g) baking powder

1 tablespoon (18 g) salt

1 cup (235 ml) buttermilk

FOR THE BISCUIT SANDWICHES:

2½ pounds (1.1 kg) loose Breakfast Sausage (see page 43)

Local honey

METHOD

1. Make the biscuits: Dice the butter into ½-inch (1 cm) cubes. Return it to the fridge.

2. In a large bowl, mix the flour, baking powder and salt together.

3. Cut the cold butter into flour mixture, mixing it with your hands until the butter is broken down into pebble-sized pieces.

4. Add the buttermilk and, using your hands, mix by folding the mixture over and over again, until you begin to notice flaky layers. Only mix until the flour and buttermilk are combined. Don't be afraid of large chunks of butter that are likely to remain in the dough. That's a good thing!

5. Using your hands, spread out the dough on a floured surface to a 1-inch (2.5 cm) thick patty. Using a 3-inch (7.6 cm) diameter ring mold, cut out biscuits and transfer them to a baking sheet. Once filled, put the baking sheet into the refrigerator, uncovered, to cool for at least 30 minutes or up to 12 hours or freeze for later use.

6. Make the biscuit sandwiches: Using ¼ pound (115 g) of sausage at a time, pat the sausage into a disc that's roughly ¼-inch (0.6 cm) thick. Transfer to a baking sheet and continue until you've formed 12 sausage patties.

7. Preheat the oven to 350°F (180°C). Bake the biscuits for 20 minutes, rotating every 5 minutes to ensure even cooking.

8. Add the sausage to the oven when 10 minutes remain on the biscuits while you do your second rotation.

9. When 5 minutes remain, brush the top of the biscuits with melted butter.

10. Make sure the biscuits are golden and the sausage is browned before removing them from the oven.

11. Using a serrated knife, slice each biscuit in half. Drizzle honey on the bottom half and then place a sausage patty on top of the honey. Replace the top half of the biscuit and enjoy.

Very Southern Mortadella and Pimento Cheese Sandwich

YIELD: 4 SANDWICHES

As elementary as a bologna cheese sandwich may sound, it's difficult to dispute the deliciousness of such a nostalgic childhood lunchtime staple. So why not bring it back, but make it better than ever? Kick that square of processed yellow to the curb, and instead invite a classic Southern cheesy spread to join the fun. Amp up the flavor of regular ole bologna by adding some smoky bacon and sweet, smooth whiskey to your pink deli meat. Then get things almost as hot as Alabama on the Fourth of July by frying it up and squishing it between two toasted buns. You're going to feel so much Southern love, you'll be licking your lips for some sweet tea and tapping your toe to bring on the banjo music.

FOR THE PIMENTO CHEESE
Makes 2 cups (500 g)

1 cup (115 g) shredded Cheddar cheese

1 cup (115 g) shredded Colby cheese

½ cup (115 g) mayonnaise

¼ cup (45 g) diced pimentos or roasted red peppers

2 tablespoons (18 g) pickled jalapeños, diced

2 tablespoons (30 ml) pickled jalapeño juice

Salt and pepper, to taste

4¼- inch (11 cm) slices Tennessee Mortadella (see page 90)

4 burger buns, slice in half

Melted butter, for toasting

METHOD

1. Preheat the oven to 350°F (180°C).

2. Heat a large skillet over medium-high heat.

3. Make the pimento cheese: Mix all of the pimento cheese ingredients together in a large bowl. Set aside.

4. Make the sandwiches: Butter both the sliced side of your burger bun and the outside. Set both sides of the bun, face down, on the center rack of the oven to toast for 3 minutes.

5. Meanwhile, add sliced bologna to the hot skillet and fry it on both sides until browned around the edges, about 2 minutes per side.

6. Spread pimento cheese on the top half of the toasted bun, put fried bologna on the bottom half, and press both sides together. Enjoy!

Irish "Bangers 'n Mash" with Onion Gravy

YIELD: 4 SERVINGS

At its simplest, bangers and mash is just that—sausage and mashed potatoes—but it doesn't have to be. To the uneducated plebeians with whom you might be caught eating, this meal seems like a very simple and unchallenging dish to prepare, but with a couple of easy tweaks, bangers 'n mash will go from drab to fabulous. For this recipe we added richness and flavor to our potatoes with a sizeable pad of butter and some silky cream, and we upped the classiness by running the potatoes through a ricer, making them perfectly smooth. Finally, the addition of traditional onion gravy topped off with a sprinkle of chives gives these freshly homemade Irish Bangers and Mash the right amount of flare for some newfound fancy friends.

4 Irish Bangers (see page 53)

Minced fresh chives

FOR MASH

3 medium Russet potatoes

1 tablespoon (18 g) salt

¼ cup (56 g) butter

¼ cup (60 ml) cream

Salt and pepper, to taste

FOR GRAVY

2 tablespoons (28 g) butter, divided

1 small onion, minced

1 teaspoon fresh thyme, minced

2 tablespoons (15 g) flour

2 cups (475 ml) beef stock

Salt and pepper, to taste

METHOD

1. Preheat the oven to 350°F (180°C).

2. Make the mash: Peel the potatoes.

3. Add the potatoes to a large stockpot and add 1 tablespoon (18 g) salt. Fill the pot with water until the potatoes are covered by 2 inches (5 cm).

4. Bring the water to a boil. Boil the potatoes for 10 to 15 minutes until they are knife tender.

5. Put the Irish Bangers onto a sheet tray and cook them in the oven for 12 to 15 minutes, until they reach the desired doneness.

6. Make the gravy: In a small stockpot over medium heat, add the butter and the onion. Sweat the onion until translucent. Add the thyme and simmer until aromatic. Sprinkle the flour over the onion mixture and cook for 1 minute, stirring occasionally. Slowly whisk in the stock, being sure to continue to whisk with each addition. Cook on low heat until it reaches the desired thickness. Season with salt and pepper.

7. Strain the potatoes through a colander and put them in a stockpot. Put the potatoes in the oven for 5 minutes. Remove and rice the potatoes in a food mill.

8. To the hot stockpot, add ¼ cup (56 g) butter and ¼ cup (60 ml) cream, and allow the butter to melt.

9. Return the potatoes to the pot with the butter and cream. Using a large spoon or spatula, mix the potatoes with the butter and cream, and then add salt and pepper to taste. (Make sure to not over-mix the potatoes or they will become gummy.)

10. Serve the sausages and mashed potatoes both drizzled with onion gravy and garnished with chives.

Italian Cotechino and Lentils

YIELD: 4 SERVINGS

It seemed fortuitous that we chose to clean out our large freezer just four days before New Year's Eve in 2014. While digging through the frozen depths of Meat Mountain, we discovered frostbitten meatballs, made space for upwards of 40 giant turkeys, and best of all, got our hands on a long lost, admittedly forgotten, vacuum-sealed package of pig skin—not a football. Cotechino and lentils might sound like an odd dish to enjoy at such a festive time as the New Year, but the beauty of this dish is that every element promises all sorts of success for the year to come. Pigs, fat as they are, are said to represent prosperity (not weight gain), and lentils are coin-shaped, which signify money. Pair your meal with a bottle of chilled Italian Prosecco, and your New Year's Eve holds the promise of prosperity, wealth, and lots of bubbles and fun.

1 tablespoon (15 ml) grapeseed or vegetable oil

1 small onion, small dice

1 medium carrot, small dice

4 cloves garlic, minced

1 teaspoon fresh thyme

1 cup (192 g) green lentils, rinsed

2 cups (475 ml) pork or chicken stock

2 pounds (910 g) Cotechino (see page 60), in 4 links

FOR THE SALAD

1 teaspoon Dijon mustard

1 whole lemon, juice only

1 tablespoon (15 ml) olive oil

1 fennel bulb, very thinly sliced

1 small red onion, very thinly sliced

1 bunch of fresh parsley, washed and picked

Salt and pepper, to taste

METHOD

1. Preheat the oven to 350°F (180°C).

2. In a medium pot, heat the oil over high heat. Sauté the onion and carrot for 2 minutes, and then add the garlic. Cook for 1 minute more, and then add the thyme, lentils, and stock.

3. Reduce the heat to low and cover the pot with a lid. Cook for 5 minutes, turn off the heat, and then let sit for 20 minutes, allowing the water to fully absorb.

4. Place the Cotechino on a baking sheet with a lip. Roast for 15 minutes in the oven, until golden brown.

5. Make the salad: In a medium-sized bowl, whisk the mustard, lemon juice, and olive oil together. Add the fennel, red onion, and parsley, and toss. Season with salt and pepper. Set aside.

6. Once the lentils and sausage are done cooking, scoop ½ cup (96 g) of the lentils into a shallow bowl. Place one Cotechino link on top and garnish with a quarter of the salad mixture.

Game Day Gumbo

YIELD: 8 SERVINGS

As guys, we are pretty much required to both love sports and love watching them regularly, but for us the best reason for watching sports or making a big deal about any particular game is that it gives us license to eat good food and drink good beer. What better way is there to spend a weekend than drinking an ice cold beer while cooking a batch of gumbo, and then drinking an ice cold beer while eating a bowl of gumbo? The oven-based, dark-hued roux, paired with our smoky Andouille sausage, imparts some incredible depth and richness to this hearty concoction, and makes it even more perfect for a cool fall day in the peak of football season. It almost makes us want to root for the New Orleans Saints.

½ cup (60 g) flour

½ cup (112 g) butter

1 pound (455 g) Andouille, sliced into coins (see page 80)

1 pound (455) chicken, diced (preferably boneless skinless thighs)

1 large onion, small dice

2 ribs of celery, small dice

2 red bell peppers, small dice

8 cloves of garlic, minced

½ pound (225 g) okra, sliced

1 can (15 ounces [420 g]) diced tomatoes

1 teaspoon fresh thyme

4 bay leaves

1 tablespoon (7 g) gumbo file powder

Dash of cayenne pepper

Dash of smoked paprika

Salt and pepper, to taste

2 quarts (2 L) chicken stock

1 pound (455 g) shrimp, peeled and deveined

METHOD

1. Preheat the oven to 300°F (150°C).

2. In a bowl, mix the flour and butter together and put in a Pyrex dish or small casserole. Bake in the oven until the color reaches a very dark brown. (This could take anywhere from 30 minutes to 2 hours, depending on how dark you want it. This is your roux. It should be near chestnut in color.)

3. Heat a large stockpot over medium-high heat. Add the sausage and cook for 2 minutes. Add the chicken and cook until both the chicken and sausage are golden brown. Remove from the pot and reserve for later. Do not discard any rendered fat from the sausage and chicken.

4. Add the onion, celery, bell peppers, and garlic to the pot with the rendered fat and sauté until softened.

5. Add the roux and all of the remaining ingredients to the stock-pot, except for the browned meat and shrimp.

6. Turn the heat down to low. Simmer for 1 hour over low heat, stirring occasionally to prevent sticking on the bottom.

7. Add the chicken, sausage, and shrimp and cook for an additional 15 minutes.

8. Serve as is or over rice.

Nashville Hot Chicken Pasta

YIELD: 4 SERVINGS • 2 LINKS NASHVILLE HOT CHICKEN SAUSAGE, SMOKED, SLICED INTO COINS (SEE PAGE 92)

"Hot Chicken" is an especially spicy variety of fried chicken that has gained notoriety across the world as Nashville's culinary claim-to-fame. Although the origin of this fiery fowl is not easily determined, what is undisputable is the way the bird is served. Chicken is breaded and deep-fried, tossed in a fire-red and cayenne-heavy sauce, served on a piece of white toast, and then stabbed with a pickle chip. In creating and cooking with our Nashville Hot Chicken Sausage, however, we like to employ a little more creativity. We substitute the pasta for white bread, garnish with parsley instead of pickles, and add cream, alcohol, and a bit of smoke to fire up your taste buds.

1 red bell pepper, diced

1 medium onion, diced

2 ribs of celery, diced

1 cup (235 ml) sherry

1 pound (455 g) bow tie pasta

1 cup (235 ml) heavy cream

1 bunch of fresh parsley, chopped

METHOD

1. In a sauté pan over medium-high heat, brown the sausage until golden and crispy around the edges.

2. Meanwhile, fill a large pot with water and bring it to a boil.

3. Add the bell pepper, onion, and celery to the pan with the sausage and sauté, stirring occasionally, until browned.

4. Deglaze the pan with the sherry. Bring the heat up and allow the liquid to reduce by half.

5. When the water has come to a rolling boil, add the pasta and cook until al dente, about 9 minutes or according to the package instructions.

6. Add the cream to the sausage and vegetable mixture and again allow the liquid to reduce by half.

7. Drain the pasta and immediately add it to the sauté pan to toss with the chicken sausage mixture. Portion a quarter of the pasta onto each plate and garnish it with fresh parsley.

Easy Chorizo Torta

YIELD: 4 SERVINGS • 1 POUND (455 G) UNSTUFFED CHORIZO (SEE PAGE 48)

Unlike the star of this recipe, the chorizo, a chorizo torta generally calls to mind the same image for all people who know and love this easy and delicious sandwich. The prep time is minimal, the ingredients are common, and the combination of hot, red chorizo and cool, green avocado will be both a delight to your eyes and to your tongue. This is one of our favorite sandwiches to make in the shop as a treat for a staff meal when there's something good to celebrate. ¡Ole!

4 large hot dog or hoagie rolls

1 head iceberg lettuce, shredded

1 tomato, sliced

1 avocado, peeled, pitted, and sliced

1 cup (230 g) sour cream

METHOD

1. Preheat the oven to 375°F (190°C).
2. Heat a large sauté pan over medium-high heat. Add the chorizo to the pan and brown, stirring occasionally.
3. Slice the buns in half, butter both halves, and toast them in the oven for 5 minutes.
4. Remove the buns from the oven and top each with a quarter of the browned chorizo. Top each sandwich with lettuce, tomato, avocado, and sour cream.

Moroccan Merguez with Couscous and Cucumber Yogurt

YIELD: 4 SERVINGS

Hailing from a part of the world where bold flavors and strong spices are beloved, it makes sense that merguez would be such a good complement to something like light and fluffy couscous. With an appearance like rice but a composition closer to pasta and a flavor that sits somewhere in between, couscous adds wonderful texture and visual interest, and it also acts as a fire extinguisher for the heat of the spicy sausage. Cucumber yogurt sauce further cools the palate and incorporates some delightful creaminess into the dish, making this meal one for the books. You'll be sure to impress guests with this simple to make, but jaw-droppingly flavorful composition. Note: The sauce can be made up to 24 hours in advance.

1 teaspoon olive oil

1 medium onion

1 large carrot

4 cups (946 ml) chicken stock

4 Merguez links (see page 74)

2 cups (350 g) dry Israeli couscous

1 tablespoon (4 g) fresh parsley, chopped

½ of an English cucumber, peeled

½ cup (115 g) plain, whole-fat or Greek yogurt

Salt and pepper, to taste

METHOD

1. Preheat the oven to 350°F (180°C).

2. In a large saucepan over low heat, add the oil, onion, and carrot and sweat for 3 to 5 minutes, until softened. Add the stock to the pan and bring it to a boil.

3. Add the merguez links to a sheet tray and roast in the oven for 12 to 15 minutes, or until desired doneness.

4. Once the chicken stock is boiling, add the couscous, stir to combine, and immediately turn off the heat. Cover the pot with a lid and let sit for 15 minutes. Fluff with a fork. Add the parsley and mix.

5. Cut the cucumber in half, lengthwise. Using a spoon, scoop out the soft flesh and set it aside. Dice the leftover firm flesh of the cucumber into small pieces. Set it aside.

6. In a small bowl, mix the cucumber components into the yogurt. Season the dressing with salt and pepper.

7. Remove the merguez from the oven and let rest for 5 minutes. Plate a quarter of the couscous in a shallow bowl. Slice the merguez on a diagonal into ¾-inch (1.9 cm) pieces and lay out on top of the couscous. Top with a dollop of the cucumber sauce.

Fried Boudin Balls with Spicy Remoulade Dipping Sauce

YIELD: 18 PIECES

People from Louisiana swear by Boudin, no matter the variety. Every individual worships his or her own special recipe and will promise you that theirs indeed reigns supreme. And though nobody can necessarily agree on which combination of ingredients is the best, they all agree that making Boudin Balls is the best way to eat it. Because what part of a fried ball of sausage dipped into a creamy and tangy sauce sounds bad? Cat's got our tongue . . .

1 pound (455 g) unstuffed Boudin (see page 88)

2 cups (240 g) flour

2 eggs

1 cup (235 ml) milk

2 cups (230 g) breadcrumbs

1 quart (1 L) lard or vegetable oil

REMOULADE

1 cup (225 g) mayonnaise

2 tablespoons (30 g) pickle relish

12 dashes hot sauce

METHOD

1. With cold, clean hands, roll the Boudin into quarter-size balls.
2. Set up three medium-sized bowls. Fill the first one with flour. In the second bowl, whisk together the eggs and milk until they are well mixed. Put the breadcrumbs into the third bowl.
3. Roll the Boudin balls in the flour until they are fully coated. Then roll the floured balls in the egg mixture, and finally cover the balls with breadcrumbs and set them aside. Repeat the process until all of the Boudin is used.
4. In a small bowl, mix the mayonnaise, pickle relish, and hot sauce together for the remoulade. Set it aside.
5. In a Dutch oven or deep cast-iron skillet, heat the lard to 350°F (180°C).
6. Working in batches of five, gently place the Boudin balls in the hot lard and fry until they are golden brown, about 4 to 5 minutes. If the fat is too shallow to cover an entire ball, turn the balls once the immersed side is golden.
7. Using a slotted spoon, remove the golden Boudin balls from the oil and set them aside on a paper towel.
8. Dip the fried Boudin balls in the spicy remoulade and enjoy!

Beer-Braised Bratwurst with Yellow Mustard and Sauerkraut

YIELD: 4 SERVINGS

Braising bratwursts in beer is a great way to add even more moisture and flavor to these already-perfect links, but the down side is that after doing so they look kind of like a giant, dead worm. Yikes. To make them flavorful and appealing to the eye—don't forget, you eat with your eyes first—we suggest two important things: good beer and a hot pan. Instead of grabbing a whole case of the light stuff, choose a six-pack of something flavorful, hearty, and delicious. You get to drink two of the six anyway. Finally, use a screaming hot pan to brown both sides of the brat to give it some color and curb-appeal; the moisture from the beer will keep it from sticking.

6-pack of your favorite local pale ale, such as Yazoo Pale Ale from Nashville

4 Bratwursts (see page 65)

4 large hot dog buns

Yellow mustard

Sauerkraut

METHOD

1. Pour 4 of the beers into a large stockpot, turn the heat to high, and bring the beer to a boil. Enjoy the two other beers by drinking them.

2. Add the bratwursts and bring the beer to a simmer. (Make sure the beer doesn't re-boil or the bratwursts may burst.)

3. Separately, heat a large sauté pan over high heat.

4. Once the bratwursts float, remove them from the beer and add them to the hot pan. Sear the bratwursts on both sides until golden.

5. Toast the buns.

6. Put the bratwursts in the buns, spread one half of the bun with the mustard, and top the brat with more mustard and sauerkraut.

Roasted Currywurst with Spätzle and Braised Cabbage

YIELD: 4 SERVINGS

With "curry" at the forefront of the word, currywurst might call forth to mind the vibrant flavors and traditional dishes of India, due to the country's love for and common use of curry in its cuisine. This version of currywurst, however, originates from a different country entirely. The "wurst" portion of this sausage hails from Germany and therefore pairs well with those tiny little spätzle dumplings and braised red cabbage. Best of all, this recipe for spätzle hails straight from the lion's mouth: James' German mother-in-law.

4 Currywurst links (see page 68)

FOR BRAISED CABBAGE

1 small head of red cabbage, cored and shredded

2 ounces (59 ml) red wine

1 ounce (29.6 ml) apple cider vinegar

1 tablespoon (20 g) honey

FOR SPÄTZLE

1 cup (120 g) flour

1 teaspoon salt

½ teaspoon ground white pepper

½ teaspoon ground nutmeg

2 large eggs, whisked

¼ cup (60 ml) milk

¼ cup (56 g) butter

2 tablespoons (8 g) fresh parsley

2 tablespoons (6 g) fresh chives

2 tablespoons (8 g) fresh tarragon

Salt and pepper, to taste

METHOD

1. Preheat the oven to 350°F (180°C).

2. Make the braised cabbage: In a medium-sized pot, add all of the ingredients for the cabbage and mix. Simmer, covered, over medium-low heat for 45 minutes, or until the cabbage is tender.

3. Fill a medium stockpot with water and bring it to a boil.

4. Make the spätzle: In a bowl, mix the flour, salt, pepper, nutmeg, eggs, and milk together with a spatula until just combined. (Be sure not to overwork.)

5. Scrape the dough onto a perforated pan or into a colander with holes no smaller than the diameter of a #2 pencil. Working directly over the pot of boiling water, scrape the dough with a spatula until little balls of the dough fall through into the boiling water below. Continue scraping the dough until all of it has gone through. (If you don't have an appropriate colander or perforated pan, you can alternatively use a large zipper-lock bag. Simply scrape all of the dough into a bottom corner of the bag and twist the top like you would a pastry bag. Snip a small hole in the corner of the bag and carefully squeeze out small ribbons of dough (no longer than 1 inch [2.5 cm]) into the pot of boiling water. You'll want to move quickly so as to allow the spätzle to cook more or less at the same rate, since the bag method is much slower.)

6. Boil the spätzle until it floats to the top of the water. Using a slotted spoon, remove the spätzle and set it aside to cool in a colander, allowing any remaining water to drain off.

7. Put the currywurst on a sheet tray and roast it in the oven for 12 to 15 minutes, or until it reaches the desired level of doneness.

8. In a large sauté pan over medium-high heat, melt the butter. Add the spätzle and sauté until it begins to color, about 1 to 2 minutes. Add the herbs and toss to combine.

9. On each of four plates, place one-fourth of the spätzle and top with one roasted currywurst and braised cabbage.

Grilled Kielbasa with Roasted Potatoes and Chimichurri

YIELD 4 TO 6 SERVINGS

Originating in Argentina, chimichurri is a fresh, herb-and-garlic-flavored sauce that makes a lovely accompaniment to meat. Although many people choose to use chimichurri as a marinade for meat, we like to let the flavors of the meat be the star and let the chimichurri take on a supporting role. By grilling the kielbasa instead of pan-frying or oven-roasting it, the sausage will get a nice crust and smoky char on the outside, flavors that go perfectly with the earthy yet bright chimichurri. Use your roasted potatoes to mop up any leftover green goodness. It's too delicious to rinse down the sink!

2 tablespoons (30 ml) grapeseed oil

2 pounds (910 g) Fingerling potatoes

Salt and pepper, to taste

4 Kielbasa links (see page 44)

FOR CHIMICHURRI

½ cup (120 ml) grapeseed oil

½ cup (30 g) chopped fresh parsley

½ cup (32 g) chopped fresh oregano

¼ cup (40 g) chopped garlic

1 teaspoon red pepper flakes

2 tablespoons (30 ml) red wine vinegar

Salt and pepper, to taste

METHOD

1. Preheat the oven to 400°F (200°C) and preheat the grill to medium heat, around 350°F (180°C).

2. Pour the oil into a large bowl. Add the potatoes, season with salt and pepper, and mix to coat.

3. Put the potatoes onto a sheet pan with a lip, placing the cut sides face down. Roast the potatoes until they are golden, about 45 minutes.

4. Make the chimichurri: In a medium-sized bowl, mix together all of the ingredients for the chimichurri. Set it aside.

5. Grill the Kielbasa for 12 to 15 minutes until cooked through and crispy on the outside.

6. Plate the potatoes, top each plate with one kielbasa link, and garnish with ample amounts of chimichurri.

9 O'clock Italian Pasta

YIELD: 4 SERVINGS

When James gets home after a late night at work, this pasta is one of his standby go-to options. It's both quick and easy, plus it requires mostly staple ingredients, meaning he can whip it up when he walks in the door around 8:30 and have it on the table by 9—with no additional trip to the grocery store necessary. After a long, hard day at work, the last thing anybody wants to do is make special stops and then slave away in the kitchen for a good dinner. Nine O'clock Italian Pasta alleviates thinking, stressing, and worst of all, eating something sub-par. Plus, it makes us feel just a little bit Italian for eating so late in the first place!

1 pound (455 g) loose Italian sausage (see page 47)

1 medium onion, diced

8 cloves garlic, minced

1 can (28 ounces, [794 g]) crushed tomatoes

1 pound (455 g) pasta, such as spaghetti

2 sprigs fresh basil, chopped

2 sprigs fresh oregano, chopped

Parmesan cheese, to taste

METHOD

1. In a medium-sized pot over medium-high heat, brown the sausage.

2. Meanwhile, bring a large pot of salted water to a boil.

3. Add the onion and garlic and sauté until they are translucent.

4. Add the crushed tomatoes and simmer for 10 minutes.

5. While the tomatoes are simmering, add the pasta to the boiling water and cook until al dente, according to the package instructions. Strain the pasta through a colander.

6. Add the herbs to the pasta sauce and mix well.

7. Put a quarter of the pasta into a shallow bowl, and ladle a quarter of the sauce on top. Grate the desired amount of fresh Parmesan on top, and serve hot.

HOBART
FARM FRESH BACON
PRB
LUNCH MENU
[SOUP]
CHICKEN & VEGGIE $5
"our signature"
FRENCH DIP - $12
OUR SLOW ROASTED ROAST BEEF, DIPPED IN BEEF JUS, TOPPED WITH BRAISED ONION & KENNY'S SWISS ON A BJH HOAGIE ... PLUS A SIDE OF JUS FOR-DIPPIN'!
PORK TONGUE SAND. - $12
BRAISED & PULLED PORK TONGUE, HAND-CUT SLAW, GREEN ONION, PICKLED JALAPEÑO, FRESH CILANTRO, & GRAINY MUSTARD ON A BJH HOAGIE.
THE REUBEN - $12
OUR HOUSE CORNED BEEF, KENNY'S SWISS, HOUSE-MADE KRAUT & 1000 ISLAND, ON BJH MARBLE RYE.
BOLOGNA N' PIMENTO - $10
FRIED PRB BEEF BOLOGNA, OUR FAMOUS PIMENTO CHEESE, & A TOASTED BJH BURGER BUN: SIMPLE, CLASSIC, PERFECT.
GRILLED CHEESE - $5
KENNY'S FARMHOUSE CHEDDAR & COLBY ON BJH SOURDOUGH. LIKE MAMA'S ... BUT BETTER.

TO PORTER ROAD BUTCHER
ANIMAL BUTCHER, FEATURING LOCALLY
AISED ANIMALS. SPECIFIC CUT VARY
RE HAPPY TO SUGGEST ALTERNATIVES.

About Porter Road Butcher

Here at Porter Road Butcher, we are passionate about providing Nashvillians with the best product available. Our meat is both healthier and better tasting because of the natural lives that our animals lived, and even the appearance of the meat tells the story of a happy life: beautiful marbling, bright vivid color, and firm, shapely cuts.

During their lives on the farms, our cows eat grass like they were intended to do, our chickens live on a green pasture blanketed by plenty of sunshine and outfitted with protection from predators, and our pigs root and forage and play around in the mud just like they do over at Old MacDonald's Farm. Never would our animals ever come from someplace like a concrete lot. No way!

We know that happy animals are the best animals, and we therefore make sure all of our animals have had the best lives possible—with just one bad day at the end of it.

By forming relationships with our farmers, we create both bonds of trust and levels of friendship,

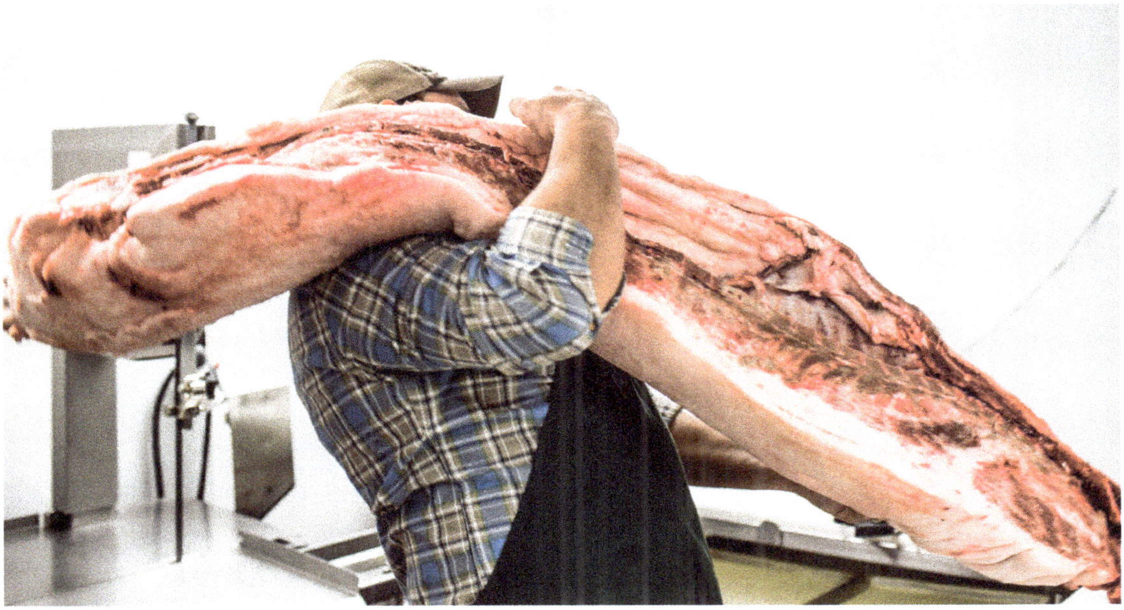

therefore holding one another accountable for the best possible product that we can then deliver to you, our friends and customers.

Keeping in line with Porter Road Butcher's mission to provide the freshest and most natural meats available, we make our sausages, pâtés, bone stocks, prepared foods, breakfast, lunch, and even dog food completely from scratch, always using the freshest ingredients available. Because, why would we use anything less?

First and foremost, quality is the driving force behind everything that Porter Road Butcher does. As a business that is owned and operated by two culinarians, Chris Carter and James Peisker, and staffed by a bunch of food-loving employees, passion and creativity are mixed into everything we do, continually increasing the quality of our work.

As a rule, we source our animals from no farther than three hours outside of our shops, and we aim to use local produce when available. Our dairy comes from a local dairy farmer, our eggs from a local egg farmer, our cheese from a small local farm with pasture-raised animals, and our market products are sourced exclusively from the region. We will stamp our name on nothing less than excellence.

How It All Began

It was a Thursday night at one favorite Nashville restaurant, and it was the first time that Chris Carter and James Peisker met. Chris was manning the meat station and James was in charge of fish, and a conversation naturally developed as the tickets started firing and the kitchen began to heat up. Before their first night of work together was over, they had formed a funny and friendly camaraderie.

As time wore on and the two spent more time together in the kitchen, James and Chris began to realize quite a few similarities between the two of them: similar work style, similar quirky senses of humor, and similar disdain for their current jobs. One sunny afternoon, Chris was driving to work and spotted a restaurant space for sale. An idea struck him and he proposed starting a business with James. Eager for a change and hungry for more creative freedom, James hopped on board, and from that moment forward, the two were business partners.

While dreaming of their own restaurant space, Chris and James noticed an emerging trend in the culinary world and soon chose to bring said trend to Nashville: artisanal butcher shops. "Lindy and Grundy was about to cut the ribbon for their shop in Los Angeles, the Butcher & Larder had just opened their doors in Chicago, and we figured we could open up a butcher shop for a sixth of the price of what we were initially looking at, and then put that money toward our restaurant space once we had enough saved," said James.

It Made Perfect Sense

The guys searched Nashville up and down for the right spot to plant their inaugural shop, but getting all of their ducks in a row required a lot of work—much more than they anticipated.

While they looked for brick-and-mortar, the soon-to-be Butcher Boys got the business going: farmers dropped off hogs to their commercial rent-a-kitchen downtown where they had enough space to entirely break down the animal; then they set up a booth at the Farmer's Market to sell fresh meat and sausage on the weekends.

"It was ridiculous," said Chris. "We would be breaking down an entire pig while the women in the kitchen space next to us were preparing lasagna and brownies and stuff."

Initially the two envisioned their shop settled in a small space located at the intersection of Porter Road and Greenwood Avenue in East Nashville, hence the name "Porter Road Butcher." But even though Chris lived just down the street and it was there that the boys set up their first [very primitive] office (complete with financial projections and amateur blueprints stapled to the walls) the space at Porter Road didn't work out. Disappointed, they kept looking.

While Chris worked the morning shift at neighborhood favorite spot Mitchell's Deli, James worked at neighboring Watanabe Japanese restaurant during dinner, affording them one person to be working at the butcher shop around the clock. Whether that meant trimming hedges and mowing lawns to earn extra dough, meeting with investors to squeeze out another drop of money, flexing their culinary muscles by booking catering events, or doing other manly-man work, there was no rest for the weary when it came to bringing their idea to fruition.

It was James who drove past Tom's Elite Barbecue, located on a bustling Gallatin Avenue in East Nashville, at the very moment they officially closed their doors and put a "for rent" sign in their window. The location, he decided, was perfect and before they knew it, Chris and James were shaking hands and signing on the dotted line.

Despite the Gallatin Road location, they kept the name, "Porter Road Butcher" and ran with it. There's a certain ring to it, don't you think? Fortunately, business at the shop has taken off, despite the somewhat confusing name, and has only become stronger, bigger, and better since their doors opened in November of 2011.

In preparation for opening up their first butcher shop, Chris and James drove all over middle Tennessee to meet with famers, tour their operations, and learn about their farming practices to find the right sources for meat that they'd be proud and excited to sell.

What they ended up with was this: beef from Bethpage, Tennessee; chicken from Ashland City, Tennessee; hogs and eggs from Summertown, Tennessee; lamb from Chattanooga; and cheese from all over the state and region.

Their operation has expanded since those early days, and they now own two butcher shops (the original in East Nashville and the newer shop in West Nashville) as well as a slaughterhouse and processing facility just an hour and a half north in Princeton, Kentucky. In an effort to continue improving the presence of their business and the quality of their products, gaining a larger audience in Nashville and acquiring the ability to control the meat from the beginning to the end were paramount in changing the face of the Nashville food industry.

And although they are growing, to this day they stand by their foundational values and the roots upon which they were grown: all local, all free-range, all truly natural, and all delicious.

About the Authors

CHRIS CARTER. Growing up in Hendersonville, Tennessee, Chris Carter was raised to love food. "It was my Granny who cooked dinner for me most of the time, and she spoiled me when it came to food," said Chris. "Dinner for the two of us could be strip steaks with eggs, plus cabbage, green beans, mashed potatoes, cauliflower, broccoli, beans. It was awesome. I think that was what got me started on liking food, but I didn't really fall in love with it until later on."

Like many other kids looking for extra spending cash, Chris's entry into the restaurant industry began in high school when he procured a job as a host and busboy for a Mexican chain restaurant. He didn't exactly enjoy his first restaurant gig as much as he would others down the road, but it was the spark that began a long string of food industry jobs and eventually a successful career.

While in college at the University of Memphis, Chris was known among his friends for his superior skills on the grill and even garnered fame among his friends for his original BBQ dry rub. Even so, his passion for food didn't run much deeper than that. It was when he was working at a liquor store and first learned about wine pairings that his ears perked up and his interest in food developed.

"I get to drink wine and eat food, and then by putting the two together make everything better?" he said. "What a great excuse."

It was then that he landed on his college major, Hospitality Management, and soon graduated with a bachelor's degree. Throughout his college years, Chris held a variety of jobs as both a bartender and a server, but he finally decided to plunge into the cooking side of things in 2006 when he attended Le Cordon Bleu College of Culinary Arts in Scottsdale, Arizona.

Living in one of the United States' wealthiest cities, high quality was something that restaurants in Scottsdale demanded, and it was there that Chris came to really appreciate the value of high-quality ingredients and being able to cook with beautiful and fresh local produce as well as obscure game such as bison.

Eventually seeking a change, Chris transitioned to a more corporate environment, Flemings Steakhouse, where his previous amateur expertise on the grill really shone and became even stronger. It was there that he actually perfected the art of grilling.

"People would come in there and spend close to $100 on a steak," he said. "I couldn't afford to mess that up."

Family matters brought Chris back to Nashville in 2009 where he quickly found work in a fine dining restaurant, and after a year met James Peisker, his soon-to-be business partner.

Today Chris lives in Nashville with his wife, Kelly, and their dogs, Marley and Clark. Outside of cooking for his family and cutting meat in the shop, Chris enjoys going fishing, the Grateful Dead, and occasionally dabbling in hot yoga.

JAMES PEISKER. "I guess I always had somewhat of an interest in food. My number one favorite toy when I was little was my fast-food restaurant play set, and my grandmother always likes to remind me how I was eager to stand on a stool in the kitchen and help her bake brownies at age five. Almost three decades later, I'm still exploring the culinary world."

A St. Louis native, James Peisker landed his first official restaurant job as a host for Layton's Diner when he was just fourteen years old. He woke up before the sun every Saturday and Sunday to usher customers to their seats and pour caffeine into their cups so he could walk out the door with some extra cash. He continued working in restaurants throughout his high school career, landing positions in both the front of the house and the back, but it was at The Gatesworth in St. Louis where James' mentor Brian Hardy instilled in him the foundation of his culinary education and whet his appetite for continuously learning more about food.

At Hardy's insistence, James pushed culinary boundaries, and he eventually decided it was time to go play with the big dogs: The Culinary Institute of America in Hyde Park, New York. Although not the biggest fan of high school, James was enamored with culinary school and took it upon himself to become the "teacher's pet" of his class. In addition to heading a variety of clubs and going the extra mile in the kitchen, James spent his free time learning how to butcher animals and properly cut meat.

When he graduated from CIA and returned to St. Louis, James worked his way up to being the rounds man in the kitchen of an upscale country club, meaning he essentially worked every station in the kitchen. After a while however, he found himself hungry for novelty, ingenuity, and challenge. He landed a position at one of the city's newest and trendiest restaurants, Niche, and subsequently found his niche in the booming St. Louis culinary scene.

The pig head terrine, a very popular dish at Niche, required whole-hog butchering, which meant that James was thrown onto the butcher block with his eyes closed. He initially faked and fudged his way through the execution but soon learned the proper method to breaking down a whole hog and found that he enjoyed it. Subsequently, butchering animals and working with meat became a passion, and he was able to share his skills with a number of the restaurants in the Craft Restaurant Group.

When James moved to Nashville with his then-girlfriend in 2010 and met his eventual business partner, Chris Carter, it seemed like a no brainer that the two would work together due to their similarities: a passion for food, a love for meat, a soft spot for good whiskey, and a dedication to a high-quality kitchen.

Today James lives in Nashville with his wife, Marta, and his two dogs, Asti and Oban. He loves reading books about food and the industry, enjoys cooking for his wife and friends, and is currently training for his first full marathon.

About the Writer

Unlike most people who live in Nashville today, **MADDIE TEREN** is a native Nashvillian who was born and raised in Music City, Tennessee, and still resides there today. The daughter of a successful songwriter, her father George passed down the writing gene to his daughter, but the desire to put that skill toward music did not, unfortunately, make the generational jump. Instead of writing songs, Maddie found that she enjoyed writing about food and began her first food blog when she was studying in Barcelona during college. Her friends were certain she was going to come home 30 pounds (14 kg) heavier. She did not.

As a kid who was nearly impossible to feed, Maddie's friends and family found it ironic that she grew into someone who not only enjoyed writing about food, but that she was also a person who was willing to try almost anything—at least once. When she returned from Barcelona to her small, college town of Oxford, Ohio, she continued writing her blog but was constantly on the hunt for exciting, interesting, and delicious food. Fortunately, back at home, Nashville was all the while growing, expanding, and morphing into a food-lover's paradise, ripe for the pickin'.

Maddie graduated from college in 2012, armed with degrees in both communication and Spanish, and initially had trouble finding a job that she felt was the right fit. So, to bide some time, earn money, and continue furthering her knowledge of food and the culinary industry, she waited tables and kept up with her blog via cooking, baking, going out to eat, and always, always writing. Eventually one thing led to another, and her work paid off.

It was in August 2013 when Maddie completed her first 200-hour yoga teacher training certification, leaving her both a new sense of clarity and confidence. She immediately joined the community at her favorite Nashville studio, Shakti Power Yoga, and as it turned out, one of the owners, Kelly, just so happened to be married to one of the Porter Road Butcher owners, Chris. And voilá! The connection was made.

Maddie transitioned into her new role as the PR and marketing manager at Porter Road Butcher in early 2014, acting as the voice behind all of PRB's social media, email newsletters, and "Butcher Blog" posts; she plans and helps run events both big and small; and she flexes her organizational muscles to keep everybody's heads on straight. The role for which she is most fond, however, is clearly being the ghost writer for *Homemade Sausage Making for Beginners*, translating James' and Chris' words, recipes, and humor into a real, live book!

Outside of the butcher shop, Maddie loves to be outdoors, whether it's riding her bike, swimming in any body of water, or drinking a good beer on a sunny patio. She also teaches three to five hot yoga classes per week and practices almost every day.

Index

V

W

Y

www.ingramcontent.com/pod-product-compliance
Lightning Source LLC
LaVergne TN
LVHW070824221225
827473LV00004B/5

9780760398067